元祖ライトノベルは「田舎の村の3つ4つの家族」の世界だった
―少し長いまえがき―

I

「恐怖小説が大好きで空想癖がある女の子が、裕福なご近所さんにリゾート地バースに連れてもらい、そこで出会った＜王子様＞と結ばれる。」本書の原作『ノーサンガー・アビー（Northanger Abbey）』（1817完成、1818出版）は、そんな話です。ただ、作者ジェイン・オースティン（Jane Austen 1776-1817）が生きたのは、フランス革命からナポレオン戦争の拡大と終結という動乱の時代でした。イギリスでは、大陸から続々と亡命してくる貴族たちのこと、そして続くナポレオンの進撃と後退や、病気の王と遊び人皇太子の政治的対立がニュースとなっていました。分かりにくければ、あちこちの紛争によって一億人の難民が生まれる状況下で新たに「大国」による隣国への侵攻が起こり、自国は核ミサイルに対する「防衛力」が問われ、疫病や原・材料高で経済が弱ることへの不安が募る社会情勢を思い浮かべましょう。そんななか「ホラーゲームにハマっているちょっと＜天然＞なフシギちゃんが、ご近所の厚意で軽井沢に滞在中、資産家のイケてる男子と出会ってゴールインし、そのうえ彼の実家のコネで優良企業に就職もしちゃう」ドラマとおきかえてください。

イギリスに話を戻しましょう。18世紀末から19世紀初め、それは富裕層がフランス革命の影響を恐れ、オースティン家のような中層の人々も社会動乱の飛び火に不安を感じる時代でした。また1815年にはイギリス側連合軍がフランス軍とワーテルローで戦火を交えています。ジェインの最後の完成作『説得』（1817執筆、1818出版）のヒロインが結ばれる相手はナポレオン戦争で財を築いた軍人で、『ノーサンガー・アビー』のヒロインの相手役の父は退役将軍です。その他ジェインの作品には少なからず軍人が登場します。しかしながら革命や戦争への言及はほとんどなく、登場人物の政治的信条が表立って描かれることも、若者の将来への不安や生まれながらの格差への不満が心の闇として追求されることも、また真摯な自己実現や燃え立つ野心が描かれることもありません。

当時イギリスで人気を博した文学作品には、たとえばウォルター・スコットの歴史大河小説群があります。それらは不安定な国際情勢のなかで相対的に安寧だった当時のイギリスの保守的で愛国的な気運に合致しており、いわば、某放送局が「○○の国」とむかし呼ばれた地方（領国）を舞台に作る「大河ドラマ」のようなものです（スコットランドは「地方」とは言えませんが）。その一つ『湖上の美人』（1810）はロッシーニのオペラ（_La Donna del Lago_, 1819）にまでなりました。少しあとにブロンテ姉妹が書いた『嵐が丘』（1847）や『ジェイン・エア』（1847）は、超自然のモチーフも取り込んだ愛と憎しみの物語で、今や女性作家の内面の叫びを伝える古典中の古典。また、このころの社会の底辺の人々の苦しみや人情を描いたチャールズ・ディケンズの作品も近代イギリス小説の代名詞です。

しかし考えてみてください。壮大な歴史大河ドラマや情念の復讐劇、魂が血を吐く恋の物語や悲惨な運命のお話ばかりでは読者は疲れてしまいます。戦争映画、欲望渦巻く政治劇、運命に翻

弄される悲恋、貧困層のドキュメンタリーなどは視聴者の世界と視野を広げてはくれますが、ようやく仕事や勉強を終えたあと毎日見たいものではないでしょう。むしろ、登場人物の思惑や価値観がどう絡み合ってどう落ち着くのか、誰が誰と結ばれるのかといった日常を半歩だけ出た話のなりゆきなら気軽に追えるのではないでしょうか。友人知人のなかにいそうな人たちが登場して、ときにクスッと笑わせてくれるとすればなおのことでしょう。

ジェイン・オースティンはもっぱら、「結婚話の域をでない日常」を書きました。登場人物は英雄やスパイや薄幸の美女や救貧院の孤児ではなく、読者の周りにいそうな愛すべき、憐れむべき、また愚かだったり嫌味だったりする人たちです。そのため評価の低い時代もありました。しかしそんなジェインの作品6篇は、30カ国語以上に翻訳され、繰り返し映画化やテレビドラマ化されています。そればかりか、なんと出版以来200年ものあいだ、小説そのものの版が途絶えたことがないのです。つまり、作品世界が狭いという定評にもかかわらずジェインの小説は、国も時代も超える普遍性をもっているといえましょう。夏目漱石は『文学論』で、「ジェイン・オースティンは写実の泰斗なり。平凡にして活躍せる文字を草して技神に入る」とその絶妙な味わいを認めています。

II

「田舎の村の3つ4つの家族こそ取り扱うべきものだ（"Three or four families in a country village is the very thing to work on"）。」姪のファニー・ナイトが書きとめた、ジェイン自身が小説の題材について述べた言葉です。まさに「村の結婚話」である自作を集約し、擁護するコメントです。とは言え当然ながら「結婚」は村だけの問題ではありません。一つ、ジェインが時の皇太子夫妻の夫婦関係について綴った文章を見てみましょう。

イギリス王室といえば人間くさいスキャンダルに事欠きませんが、実は当時も相当ひどかったのです。父王がポルフィリン症で精神障害をきたしたため摂政の座についた皇太子（のちのジョージ4世）は、贅沢と賭博と女性関係のため借金まみれ。国庫からの負債を棒引きしてもらうべく、同棲中のフランス人未亡人と別れてしぶしぶドイツ人の従姉キャロラインと結婚したものの、夫妻仲は最初から険悪そのものでした。皇太子は妃から皇族としての特権をはく奪し、妃もその反動からか男性の取り巻きに囲まれた生活を始めます。皇族が直接政治に関与したこの時代、皇太子夫妻そろってのイメージ失墜は政党政治にも影響しました。

ジェインは社会に無関心ではありませんでした。外国から嫁いできた妃に対してイギリスのメディアや国民が厳しい目を向けるなか、1813年2月16日に友人に宛てた手紙でジェインは妃に味方し、同性としての歯がゆさまで表しています。

Poor woman, I shall support her as long as I can, because she is a Woman, & because I hate her Husband — but I can hardly forgive her for calling herself "attached & affectionate" to a Man whom she must detest … I am resolved at least always to think that she would have been respectable, if the Prince had behaved only tolerably by her at first.

この文章からは、生前最後に出版した小説『エマ（*Emma*)』(1815)に表れる女同志の連帯感さえ感じられます。ちなみに、皇太子は、ジェインが匿名で発表していた作品の愛読者で、侍医を通した出会いでジェインが作者だと気づきました。皮肉なことにジェインは、大嫌いなこの男から「余に献じてよし」と伝えられてしまい、出版前の『エマ』を「献じる」ことになりました。（当時は出版物に「～に献じる」と有力者の名前を入れる慣習が残っており、それがプロモーションにもなりました。）

　話を戻すと、結婚は立場によっては国政にも関わる問題だ、と歴史好きのジェインはことさら心得ていたはずで、しかも「結婚の成功と失敗は運以外なにものでもない」と述べています。彼女は、もっぱら結婚話を軸にした話を書きながらも、結婚が人生を左右するような当時の社会の仕組みを快く思ってはいませんでした。しかし現実に結婚は親の身分や資産の状況や容姿に左右され、それがまた社会身分と経済の問題として女性の（そして男性の）人生を大いに左右しました。しかも多くの若者が戦地に出向くか入隊したこの時代、持参金のない女性は圧倒的に不利でした。結婚は、当事者それぞれのレベルの切迫した「政治」なのです。

　ジェインはこの現実を認め、社会と人生の問題をそこに集約したのです。そうした限定的な価値観が支配する世界に生きる人々のふるまいや会話や心理を、鋭い観察眼で静かに見てとり、

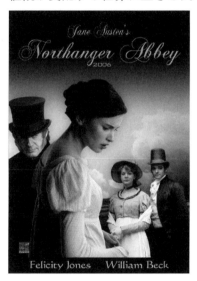

ちょっと離れて皮肉を利かせ、ユーモアで味をつけて作品にしたのです。そんな「選択と集中」、描かれる卑近な現実とそれを描く作家との絶妙な距離こそが、「世界一平凡な大作家」ジェイン・オースティンの、「田舎の村の３つか４つの家族」でなる作品の魅力だと言えましょう。

　さて本書8～10章のコラムでは、ジェイン・オースティンの人生を、その住まいの変遷をたどりつつまとめてみました。目を通していただき、またぜひ彼女が残した他の作品もお楽しみください。そうすれば、作家自身の経験とそこで出会った人たちが、含みのある語り口で小説に昇華されていることを実感し、まさに「日常にこそドラマがある」と納得されることでしょう。

Northanger Abbey retold in simple English

Chapter 6

Chapter 7

Chapter 8

Chapter 9

Chapter 10

Chapter 11

Chapter 12　　**94**

Exit Questions

原作参考資料　*Northanger Abbey, Lady Susan, The Watsons, and Sanditon* by Jane Austen
　　　　　　　（Oxford World Classics:1985）

＊英文中の◆は、Appendix の終了箇所を示しています。

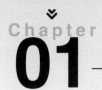

» Get ready with vocabulary!

Match the Japanese words 1〜10 with the English words given below.

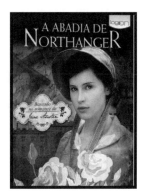

1 夢中になっている　　2 結婚する資格がある　　3 土地屋敷

4 魅力的な　　5 気まずい　　6 良くなる　　7 感じが良い

8 認める　　9 洗練されている　　10 野心

approve	pleasant	improve	sophisticated	ambition
absorbed	eligible	property	attractive	awkward

» Enjoy the story!

01 Catherine goes to Bath

Answer the following questions in Japanese as you read the story.

1 What do you know about Catherine Morland?
キャサリンはどう描かれていますか。

2 What do you know about the Morland family?
モーランド一家はどう描かれていますか。

3 What do you know about Mr. and Mrs. Allen?
アレン夫妻はどんな人たちですか。

Catherine Morland had not been special in any way. No one who had ever seen Catherine in her childhood would have thought that she was born to be a heroine. The Morlands were a family of ten children, and a family of ten children will always be called a fine family when there are heads and arms and legs enough for the number. But the Morlands were a plain family, neither rich nor poor. They happily lived in the village of Fullerton.

At the age of seventeen, Catherine had never been in love, and no one had ever

been in love with Catherine, either. Besides, in Fullerton, there were no **eligible** men. Lately, she was rather **absorbed** in reading novels.

There lived, however, Mr. and Mrs. Allen, who owned a lot of **properties** in the village.

Mr. Allen was not well and Mrs. Allen was fond of Catherine. ◆ They decided to go to the spa town of Bath and stay there for some time. Thinking that life in a small village would be boring for a young lady who should be looking for her future husband, they invited Catherine to go with them. Her parents gladly agreed. They thought that going to Bath would be a new experience for their eldest daughter. Catherine, of course, was excited. She was a cheerful, **attractive** girl, if not particularly beautiful.

02 Catherine meets Henry Tilney

Answer the following questions in Japanese as you read the story.

1 What did Mrs. Allen do before going to dance?

バースでキャサリンとダンスに行く前にアレン夫人は何をしましたか。

2 What impression did Henry Tilney leave on Catherine?

ヘンリー・ティルニーはキャサリンにどんな印象を与えましたか。

3 Why did Henry Tilney know well about ladies' clothes?

ヘンリー・ティルニーが女性の衣服についてよく知っているのはなぜですか。

In Bath, before going to dance, Mrs. Allen prepared new gowns* both for herself and for Catherine at a fashionable shop. Mrs. Allen's main interest was in fine clothes.

But at the first dance, though there were so many people in the Ball Room*,

Introduced......at "Mr Henry Tilney."

they could not find any acquaintances. Mrs. Allen and Catherine felt a little **awkward** for a while. "I want to find a partner for you, Catherine, but maybe another evening," said Mrs. Allen.

After the dancing had finished, however, some gentlemen noticed Catherine and said that she was pretty in a loud voice, which **improved** the evening very much for her.

Mr. and Mrs. Allen and Catherine moved to the Pump Room*. There, things turned more interesting to Catherine. A young handsome man bumped into Mrs. Allen by accident, had an eye on Catherine, and asked the master of ceremonies* to introduce himself to her. His name was Henry Tilney.

Thus, formally introduced to each other, they danced and talked together. She found the young man very **pleasant**, and intelligent, too. He had a sister very close to himself, so he knew a lot about ladies' clothes. This pleased Mrs. Allen and she **approved** Henry Tilney as Catherine's proper partner.

The next day, Catherine went to the Pump Room, but Tilney was not there. Mrs. Allen said, "Bath is a lovely place, but I wish I knew more people here." Catherine had heard this from Mrs. Allen many times since their arrival in Bath. But that day Mrs. Allen's wish came true.

* gown = dress, * the Ball Room=the large room for dance
* the Pump Room = a pump house at a spa where people gather to drink medicinal waters
* the master of ceremonies: see the Column of Chapter 3

03 Catherine meets Isabella Thorpe

Answer the following questions in Japanese as you read the story.

1 What surprised Catherine?

キャサリンはなぜ驚いたのですか。

2 What was the ambition that Mrs. Thorpe held in Bath?

ソープ夫人はバースでどんな野心を抱いていたでしょうか。

3 What did Isabella encourage Catherine to do?

イザベラはキャサリンにどうするよう勧めましたか。

"Aren't you Mrs. Allen?" A lady of about the same age as Mrs. Allen sat next to her. Mrs. Allen recognized the lady. She was Mrs. Thorpe. The two ladies had not seen each other for a long time, so they talked about their children and everything. Mrs. Allen did not fail to notice that Mrs. Thorpe's lace was not so fine as hers.

Soon Mrs. Thorpe's daughters arrived. The mother introduced her daughters to Mrs. Allen and Catherine. Catherine's family name interested the eldest daughter Isabella. To Catherine's surprise, she said, "Miss Morland looks very much like her brother." But then Catherine remembered that her eldest brother James had become friends with a young man named Thorpe. Catherine was happy to make more friends in Bath.

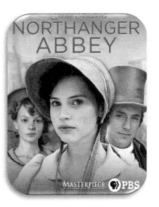

Isabella Thorpe was four years older than Catherine. She looked **sophisticated** and pretty to Catherine. They became friends quickly. Mrs. Thorpe was a widow not well off at all. She hoped her daughter Isabella would marry someone rich and help her entire family out of poverty. Indeed, Bath should have been an appropriate place for such an **ambition**.

Catherine and Mr. and Mrs. Allen went to the theatre next evening. Catherine expected to see Mr. Tilney somewhere in the theatre, but he was not to be seen anywhere. Since he had not said that he would leave Bath, he now seemed more mysterious and interesting to Catherine.

Catherine talked about Henry Tilney with Isabella, who encouraged her to stay interested in him. "I'm sure he will come back," sighed Catherine to herself.

Mrs. Allen was also happy. She now had company in Bath, and furthermore, her old friend was not so well-dressed as herself.

» Reviewing the story

I • Reorder a)~e) according to the story.

a) Catherine, introduced to Isabella Thorpe, was surprised to know that Isabella knew her brother James.

b) Catherine was introduced to Henry Tilney by the master of the ceremonies and found him pleasant.

c) Mr. and Mrs. Allen invited Catherine to Bath.

d) Mrs. Allen bought new gowns for herself and Catherine in Bath.

e) Catherine expected to find Henry Tilney at the theatre in vain.

II • Complete the sentences using the given words.

sophisticated	acquaintance	pleasant	awkward	ambition

1 Catherine and Mrs. Allen felt [   ] when they first arrived at the Ball Room.

2 Mrs. Allen found an old [   ] in the Pump Room.

3 Catherine found Henry [   ] and intelligent.

4 Isabella looked [   ] to Catherine.

5 Mrs. Thorpe had an [   ] that Isabella should marry a rich man.

» Listening and oral practices

Fill the blanks as you listen and practice the conversation with your partner.

A : Aren't you Mrs. Allen?

B : Yes. And you are···.

A : Mrs. Thorpe. [¹   ]

B : Oh, Mrs. Thorpe, of course. Excuse me for not recognizing you. [²
    ] ? How's your family?

A：Well, so many things have happened to us. I'm a widow now.

B：Oh, [³   ]. But you are not alone here, are you?

A：No. My daughters are with me. Well, in fact, I have to say we are here for [⁴   ] for my eldest daughter Isabella.

B：Oh, of course. Bath is the place for that.

» Tips for reading

◀ 直接法過去完了 ▶　形は「had + 過去分詞」。意味は「過去のある時を軸にして、その時より前に起こったり、その時に結果がでていたり、その時も、あるいは直前まで続いていた行為や状態。」

▶ 1)〜4) それぞれの軸となる過去の時を特定し日本語に訳しましょう。1) では同文中に示されていません。

1) Catherine Morland **had not been** special in any way.

2) At the age of seventeen, Catherine **had never been** in love, and no one **had ever been** in love with Catherine, either.

3) Catherine remembered that her eldest brother James **had become** friends with a young man named Thorpe.

4) Everything **had been finished** when the children came to Mrs. Tilney.（Chapter 9）

▶ 英語を完成しましょう。

1) In Bath, Mrs. Allen [   ] uncomfortable till she [   ] Mrs. Thorpe. Mrs. Thorpe [   ] a widow for some time.
   バースでは、ソープ夫人と出会うまでアレン夫人は居心地が悪かった。ソープ夫人はしばらくまえから未亡人でした。

2) Isabella [   ] James Morland before she [   ] with Catherine.
   イザベラはキャサリンと友達になる前にジェイムズ・モーランドと出会っていた。

◀ 仮定法過去完了 ▶　形は「had + 過去分詞」。意味は「過去の事実に反する仮定」
過去についての仮定から導く結論は、過去と現在の両方ありえる。
If you **had seen** Catherine in her childhood, you **would have never thought** that she was born to be a heroine.
もしあなたが子供時代のキャサリンを<u>見たなら</u>、彼女がヒロインになるべく生まれたとは<u>決して思わなかったでしょう</u>。
If Jane **had not written** her novels, some of the towns she visited **would not be known** worldwide as now. もしジェインが小説を<u>書かなかったら</u>、彼女が訪れた町のいくつかは今の

ように世界的に<u>知られてはいない</u>でしょう。

参考）◀ 仮定法過去 ▶

　　形は過去、意味は現在の事実に関する仮定。原則 be 動詞は were になる。

　　If I were Catherine, **I would** not tell Isabella about Mr. Tilney.

　　I wish I could visit Bath in the age of Jane Austen.

▶ 1）は日本語訳を 2）は英語を完成しましょう。

1）Catherine answered she liked John. **But if Catherine had not been flattered, the answer might have been different.**（Chapter 2）

　　キャサリンはジョンのことを好きだと答えました。しかし［ 　　　　　　　　　　　　　 ］。

2）**If Mrs. Allen ［ 　　　　　　　　 ］ Catherine, she ［ 　　　　　　　 ］ Mr. Tilney and she ［ 　　　　　　　　 ］ in Bath in the first place.**

　　もしアレン夫人が招待してくれなかったら、キャサリンはティルニーさんと出会わなかったし、そもそも今バースにいないでしょう。

◀ if not ▶　「でないとして（も）」

Catherine was attractive, **if not** particularly beautiful.

キャサリンは取りたてて美しくはなかったとしても魅力的でした。

▶ 英文を完成しましょう。

The Morland family were relatively well-off, ［ 　　　　　 ］.

モーランド一家はお金持ちではないにしても暮らし向きは比較的良好でした。

≫　Read a part of the original passage

　　The master of the ceremonies introduced to her a very gentleman-like young man as a partner; his name was Tilney. He seemed to be about four or five and twenty, was rather tall, had a pleasing countenance, a very intelligent and lively eye, and, if not quite handsome, was very near it. His address was good, and Catherine felt herself in high luck.

Captain William Wade, the Master of Ceremonies

≫　Write a passage as a character

Write a passage of 4~6 sentences from Catherine's diary about the first two days in Bath.

column 01 バース ― 古代からの温泉の地

『ノーサンガー・アビー』の主な舞台の一つ、イングランドのバース（Bath）は人口約9万人の観光都市でイギリス最初のアーバンリゾートです。古代ローマ支配下のころに温泉が利用され、「風呂 bath」の語源となりました。1987年にはユネスコの世界文化遺産に指定されています。

1610年のバースの地図

考古学的考察によれば、この町の3カ所の温泉源は古代ローマ以前のケルトの時代すでに民間信仰の対象だったようです。しかし中世になると温泉の存在は地元の人々以外にはしばらく忘れ

バース　古代ローマ時代の公衆浴場

られ、人口も9000人ほどとなりました。「再発見」されたのはエリザベス1世（在位1558-1603）の時代で、鉱泉の幅広い効用が知られるようになり、続いて17世紀には王妃が不妊治癒に訪れて王子を授かったことをきっかけに本格的に上流の人々の静養地となります。さらに18世紀初め、アン女王が痛風治療に通うと広い層のリゾート地として発展しました。このころになると鉱泉に身を浸すのではなく、40種類以上のミネラルを含んで湧き出る鉱水を飲むことで病気の治癒や健康増進の効力があるとされました。そしてジェインの時代を経た1880年、それまで知られていなかった源泉を使用した古代ローマの入浴場が新たに発見されます。2006年にはそれを使った新しい温泉施設がオープンしています。

街並みについてですが、今残るのは1774年から本格的に整備されたもので、まさにジェインがしばらく暮らし、また『ノーサンガー・アビー』に描いた光景です。主要な建築の設計の多くを手がけたのはジョン・ウッド（1704-1754）、ならびに同名の息子です。バースの街全体がすっきりと調和のとれた統一感を残すのは、ウッド親子が、16世紀にイタリアで活躍した新古典派建築の祖アンドレア・パッラーディオに傾倒していたからでしょう。また18世紀後半に町全体の整備が劇的に進んだ背景には、イングランドにおいて余裕のある層が厚くなり、まさに『ノーサンガー・アビー』が語るような娯楽と社交の場が求められたことがあります。

町のさらに古くからあるランドマークの一つ、バース・アビーを見ましょう。この僧院は676年にベネディクト派修道院として創建され、その後廃墟同然となるなどの困難を乗り越えて、973年にはここで初の統一イングランド王ウェセックスのエドガー王の戴冠式が行われました。

今美しさで目を引くその姿の主要部分は、1499年にオリヴァー・キング司教が再建したチューダー朝様式の建物で、暖色を帯びた柔ら

バース　パンプ・ルームのファウンテン

バース・アビー、ファッサード（部分）「天使の階段」

バース・アビー、西ファッサード

バース・アビー天井

かい色合いを持つ地元の石材「バース・ストーン」が使われています。「天使の階段」など独特の意匠を持つ優雅な西ファッサードにまず目が行きますが、「薔薇の天井」など内部の装飾も注目に値します。

　バースに数ある有名建築からもう一つだけ紹介するなら、ジョージ四世が残したロイヤル・パヴィリオンでしょう。この王の放蕩については本書「はじめに」でも触れていますが、彼はインド＝イスラム風の外観にシノワズリ（中国趣味）を加えた内装で王宮を建てました。後にそれをブライトン市がヴィクトリア女王から買い取り、陶器や調度品のコレクションとともに一般公開すると、世界中から見学者が来るようになりました。

バース、ロイヤル・パヴィリオン

バース、ロイヤル・パヴィリオン音楽室天井

　その他、多くの有名人が暮らした集合住宅ロイヤル・クレッシェンドやリージェンシー時代に遡る社交施設の数々、さらにファッション美術館などバースへの興味はつきません。ロンドンから電車で西へ約一時間半。ジェイン・オースティンが暮らし、描いたバースを、ぜひいつか皆さんも体感してみてください。

参考資料

Rick Steve's Europe "England's Bath and York"（October 7, 2006: American Public Television）
バース観光案内サイト https://visitbath.co.uk/
バース歴史サイト https://www.historic-uk.com/HistoryMagazine/DestinationsUK/Bath/

» Get ready with vocabulary!

Match the Japanese words 1～10 with the English words given below.

1 好ましい　　2 顔色　　3 秘密をばらす・裏切る

4 感心させる、（良い）印象を残す　　5 下宿・滞在先

6 喜ばしい　　7 恥じ入る　　8 （世辞などを）喜んでいる

9 気分が悪い・嫌がっている　　10 堂々として

| complexion | favourable | betray | impress | delightful |
| annoyed | ashamed | flattered | lodging | dignified |

» Enjoy the story!

01 **Catherine and Isabella become closer**

Answer the following questions in Japanese as you read the story.

1 How did Isabella Thorpe and Catherine spend time together when the weather was not so good?

天気が良くないとき、イザベラ・ソープとキャサリンは何をして時間を過ごしたでしょう。

2 What did Isabella say about *The Mysteries of Udolpho*?

『ユードルフォーの怪』についてイザベラはなんと言ったでしょう。

3 What did Isabella say that Catherine did not understand?

イザベラは、キャサリンが理解できないどんなことを言ったでしょう。

Catherine spent a lot of time with Isabella. They visited the shops on the fashionable streets in Bath arm in arm. When the weather was not **favourable** for walking, they read novels together. They spoke about the novel Catherine was reading. It was *The Mysteries of Udolpho* and Catherine was at a very exciting point of the story. Isabella said that she had already read the novel. "But I wouldn't tell you what happens next," she added. ◆

They also talked about men. "What hair colour do you like in a man?" Isabella asked at one time. "I haven't thought about that much. How about you?" Catherine asked. Isabella answered, "I prefer light eyes and **complexion**. But don't **betray** me." Catherine did not understand what Isabella meant. So she said, "Betray you?" Then Isabella answered, "Oh, I've said too much. Let' change the subject."

02 Catherine meets John Thorpe with James

Answer the following questions in Japanese as you read the story.

1 Who were on the carriage going at full speed?

フルスピードで飛ばしてきた馬車には誰が乗っていたでしょう。

2 Where did the four youths go after having greeted each other?

互いにあいさつをしてから、若者4人はどこへ行ったでしょう。

3 Why was not Catherine able to hear what Isabella and James were talking about?

なぜ、キャサリンにはイザベラとジェイムズが話していたことが聞こえなかったのでしょう。

(1-7)

One day, Isabella and Catherine were trying to cross one of the busy streets, when a carriage stopped right after passing them. It had been going at full speed. Looking up

at the carriage, Isabella's face lit up and she said, "Mr. Morland! And John!" Catherine cried, too. "Good heavens! It's James!" On the carriage were Isabella's brother John Thorpe and Catherine's brother James Morland. Catherine and James were pleased to see each other and they hugged and kissed.

John Thorpe also noticed Catherine and tried to **impress** her. "Miss Morland! What do you think of my carriage? Have you ever seen such an animal as this? We've come forty kilometres in only three and a half hours!" Then he asked where Catherine and Isabella were going. The two brothers decided to accompany their sisters to the Thorpe's **lodging** to greet Mrs. Thorpe.

"Do you like open carriages?" John Thorpe asked Catherine.

"Yes, but I don't have much opportunity to ride on them."

"Then I'll take you around in mine every day."

Catherine was at a loss and just said, "Thank you." Isabella exclaimed, "Oh, how **delightful**! But there won't be room for a third person."

John Thorpe laughed, "Oh, of course no. I haven't come to Bath to take my sister about in my carriage. James will take care of you."

Soon Isabella and James were speaking to each other. Catherine could not hear what they were talking about because John kept talking in a loud voice. He talked about horses and it was boring to Catherine. So, Catherine dared to ask, "Have you ever read *The Mysteries of Udolpho*?" "No. I don't read novels. They are so full of nonsense" was John's answer. Catherine felt **ashamed**. Then he said, "If I read a novel, it would be one by Mrs. Radcliffe. She is a very popular writer, you know." "Oh, *The Mysteries of Udolpho* was written by her," replied Catherine. John said, "Oh, was it? Then I was thinking about some other stupid books."

03 Catherine is not impressed with John Thorpe

Answer the following questions in Japanese as you read the story.

1 Why did Catherine say that she liked John Thorpe?

どうしてキャサリンは、ジョン・ソープに好感を持ったと言ったのでしょう。

2 What excuse did Isabella give on leaving Catherine alone?

イザベラは、キャサリンをひとりにするときどんな言い訳をしたでしょう。

3 Why was Catherine annoyed with John Thorpe at the dance?

キャサリンは、なぜ、ダンス場でジョン・ソープのことを嫌だと思ったのでしょう。

On their arriving at Mrs. Thorpe's lodging, she appeared and hugged her son. John said that he and his friend James were going to stay in Bath for a few days. He then commented on his mother, "You look like a witch in your bonnet," and said to his little sisters, "You are both ugly today."

Later, Isabella said to Catherine that her brother John had said that Catherine was the prettiest girl he had ever met. Catherine was **flattered**.

On the way back to Allen's lodging, James asked Catherine what she thought of John Thorpe. Well, Catherine was not impressed with John's manners at all. And if she had not been flattered, the answer might have been different. But she thought, "John Thorpe is Isabella's brother and a friend of James'." So she answered, "I like him very much." James was pleased to hear this. He went on saying how much he liked Isabella and how glad he was to know that Isabella and Catherine were friends.

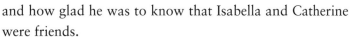

At the entrance of the lodging, James arranged to meet Catherine, Isabella and John later for the dance, and he left to go to dinner.

The four youths met at the Ball Room. As soon as the dancing began, James danced with Isabella. But John left Catherine and went to play cards. Catherine sat alone. Isabella said, "We won't leave you alone," and Catherine was grateful. But a little while later, Isabella talked to James for a minute and said to Catherine, "I'm sorry, I must leave you, because your brother is important. I'm sure John will be soon back." Catherine was **annoyed** with John not because she wanted to dance with him but because, to other people, she looked as if she had come to dance without a partner and could not find one. But Catherine sat **dignified** waiting for her partner to turn up.

❯❯ Reviewing the story

I • Reorder a)∼e) according to the story.

a) Catherine and Isabella ran into their brothers on the street.

b) Catherine came to spend a lot of time with Isabella Thorpe shopping and reading novels.

c) James Morland asked his sister how she felt about John Thorpe.

d) Catherine was left alone at the dance.

e) The four youths visited Mrs. Thorpe at her lodging.

II • Complete the sentences using the given words.

flattered	impress	ashamed	complexion	dignified

1 Isabella prefers men with light [   ].

2 John Thorpe boasted of his horse and tried to [   ] Catherine.

3 Catherine felt [   ] when John Thorpe said that novels were full of nonsense.

4 Catherine was [   ] to hear John's compliments on her from Isabella.

5 Catherine sat [   ] though she knew she looked as if she could not find a dance partner.

❯❯ Listening and oral practices

Fill the blanks as you listen and practice the conversation with your partner.

A : *The Mysteries of Udolpho*! I've already read the novel. But I won't tell you [¹   ]. By the way, what colour of hair do you like in a man?

B : [²   ]. How about you?

A : [³   ]. But don't betray me.

B : Betray you? What do you mean?

A : Oh, I've said too much. [⁴   ].

» Tips for reading

感情や状態に影響を与える他動詞

▶ 物語の英文のなかから、[　]内で最初の一文字与えられた動詞を使って次の英文を完成しましょう。

John Thorpe did not [¹ i-　　　　] Catherine with his talks on horses but [² f-　　　] her with his compliments. Later she said she liked John Thorpe and this [³ p-　　　　] James.

感情や状態に影響を与える他動詞の現在分詞・過去分詞

現在分詞（-ing）と過去分詞（-ed など）でそれぞれ能動と受動の意味を含む形容語となります。

▶ 現在分詞と過去分詞どちらか相応しい方を選びましょう。

1）In fact, to Catherine, John Thorpe was not [**interesting/interested**] at all. But his compliment was [**flattering/ flattered**]. Catherine was so [**flattering/ flattered**] that she ended up saying she liked John. James was [**pleasing/pleased**] to hear this.

2）Dancing with John will be [**tiring/tired**]. Listening to him, Catherine will feel very [**boring/ bored**].

▶ 以下は同じく感情や状況に影響を与える他動詞の例です。意味を確認しておきましょう。

amuse, awaken, charm, disappoint, dissatisfy, disgrace, despair, excite, exhaust, fascinate, frustrate, horrify, terrify, satisfy, stimulate, thrill, upset

注）**pleasing**「喜ばせる」と **pleasant = agreeable**「心地よい・感じの良い」（Chapter 1）を区別すること。

　　参考）結果（帰結）や同時を表す現在分詞

　　　　Catherine said she liked John, **pleasing** James.

　　　　キャサリンはジョンを好ましく思うと言い、ジェイムズを喜ばせた。（帰結）

　　　　Catherine finally went downstairs **dreading** what Henry would say to her. (Chapter 10)

　　　　キャサリンはようやく、ヘンリーが何を言うか恐れつつ降りてきた。（同時）

過去分詞に続く前置詞の例　be impressed with ～＝パフォーマンスや作品などに感動する、be impressed by/with～ ＝人物（の行い）などに感銘を受ける、be annoyed with/ by ～＝人の行動などを嫌がる・腹が立っている、など。

▶ 前置詞を補って英文を完成しましょう。

1）Catherine was excited [　　　　] going to Bath.

2）Catherine was not so impressed [　　　　] the speed of John's horse.

3）Catherine was not impressed [　　　　] John at all.

13

4) James was pleased [   ] Catherine's answer.

5) Catherine was annoyed [   ] John because he had left her alone at the dance.

6) Catherine felt ashamed [   ] looking as if she could not find a partner.

❯❯ Read a part of the original passage

John Thorpe (...) was a stout young man of middling height, who, with a plain face and ungraceful form, seemed fearful of being too handsome unless he wore the dress of a groom, and too much like a gentleman unless he were easy where he ought to be civil, and impudent where he might be allowed to be easy. He took out his watch: "How long do you think we have been running it from Tetbury, Miss Morland?"

❯❯ Write a passage as a character

Write a passage of 3～5 sentences from the diary of James Morland about the day he found his sister Catherine and Isabella Thorpe had become good friends.

恐怖小説の大流行

キャサリンは怖いお話に夢中です。目下のお気に入りはアン・ラドクリフの『ユードルフォーの怪』のようですね。これは1794年に出版された実在の小説で、イタリアの貴族男性がイギリス人女性を騙して、主人公であるその姪ともども北イタリアに連れ去る話です。ストーリーそのものは荒唐無稽ですが、近年は歴史や心理学の視点からの見直しが進んでいます。

The Mysteries of Udolpho 1793年版挿絵

実は18世紀後半から19世紀初めにかけて、今ゴシック小説と総称される恐怖小説が大流行していました。当時は書籍が高価なため、通常の貸本屋だけでなく、馬車で各地をまわる「巡回図書館」や「貸し出し図書室」と呼ばれる貸本屋が繁盛していました。最初の巡回図書館は1725年にスコットランドのエディンバラでアラン・ラムゼイという人が、そしてイングランドではその3年後にジェイムズ・リークという人が開きました。絵空事を描く小説流行の温床として非難を受けながらも市場を広げ、1790年代を調べたある統計によれば、貸本の品ぞろえの9割近くがゴシック小説でした。

ゴシック小説では中世ゴシック風の屋敷、古城、僧院などを舞台に超自然的なことが起こるのが常套で、人物、道具立てに一定の型がありました。たとえば、圧制的で残忍な男性

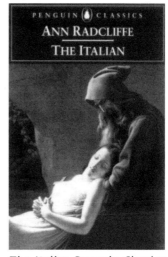

The Italian Penguin Classics
Audio 2020 配信版パッケージ

親族や修道僧に監禁されて迫害を受ける妻や娘や修道女、あるいは屋敷や財産が強奪されて苦難を味わう正統な相続人が頻繁に登場します。舞台はイタリア、フランス、スペインなどカトリックの国が主流で、迫害の一手段として宗教裁判が設定される例もあります。ただ、こうした古めかしい道具立てながら、風景描写や舞台となる建物には、自然や建築に関する当時の新しい美意識が活かされていました。

これらゴシック小説の流行の背景には、経済的に他国を抜いて逸早く市民社会を築いていたイングランドの、カトリック諸国に対する優越感や、逆に文化の伝統においてはそれらの国に後塵を拝してきたという劣等感など、イギリスの読者の複雑な政治感覚もうかがえます。革命に揺れたり旧態依然とした教会支配に苦しんだりする外国と、それに比して安定し裕福な自分たちの国。ひと時の恐怖を読書で味わったあとで恵まれた社

The Castle of Otranto ドイツ
1794年版イラスト

会にいるわが身の安寧を実感する、といった心理があったとされます。ちなみに、『ユードルフォーの怪』に関しては、小説に描かれるロンバルディの3つの城の内部と概観のようすそれぞれが幽閉される主人公や作者が社会情勢に感じていた潜在的な恐怖を反映しているといった読み解きまであります（神尾美津雄「幽霊城の内と外：ラドクリフ『ユードルフォーの神秘』）。ノーサンガー・アビーにおけるキャサリンの恐怖を滑稽に描く作者の目は時代を平静に見る目でもあったのでしょう。

　最後に恐怖小説の系譜をごく簡単に言うと、始まりはホレス・ウォルポールの『オトラント城奇譚』（1764）で、クレアラ・リーブの『老イギリス男爵』（1777）を経て1790年代に絶頂期を迎え、その代表作が先出の『ユードルフォーの怪』と同作家による『イタリア人』（1797）で、これらの作品にはいずれも迫害される女主人公が登場します。

　またフランス革命に共鳴したウィリアム・ゴドウィンの『ケイレブ・ウィリアムズ』（1794）も迫害を受ける人物を扱っています。マシュー・グレゴリー・ルイスの『修道士』（1796）はドイツ文学の影響が強く、近親相姦や親殺しも登場して「娯楽」の域を超えた感があります。加えてメアリ・シェリーの『フランケンシュタイン』（1818）やチャールズ・マチューリンの『放浪者メルモス』（1820）など、後期ゴシック小説は作者の分身的人物の創造を特色とし、書き手の目は文明や人の心の内奥と闇に向けられていきました。

　こんなふうに、ふりかえれば決して浅薄ではない系譜を持つ小説群なのですが、ジェイン・オースティンは、純朴な女の子キャサリンが安易にゴシック小説の影響を受ける姿をユーモラスに描くことでその流行を揶揄しています。自身がゴシック小説を存分に愉しんだ経験のあるジェインならではの切り口だと言えるでしょう。

Frankenstein Wordsworth Classics 2014年版表紙

Chapter

03

NORTHANGER ABBEY

❯❯ Get ready with vocabulary!

Match the Japanese words 1～10 with the English words given below.

1 かっこいい　　2 謝る　　3 会話　　4 立ち振る舞い・礼儀

5 礼儀正しく　　6 混乱　　7 疑っている　　8 制御する・対応する

9 集中する　　10 名付け親

confusion　　doubtful　　dashing　　handle　　concentrate

conversation　　manners　　politely　　godfather　　apologize

❯❯ Enjoy the story!

01 Catherine does not dance with Henry Tilney

Answer the following questions in Japanese as you read the story.

1 How did Henry Tilney look? How did the lady talking with him look?

ヘンリー・ティルニーと、彼の話し相手の女性の外見はどうだったでしょう。

2 Why did not Catherine dance with Henry?

キャサリンはどうしてヘンリーと踊らなかったのでしょう。

3 What did John Thorpe talk about while dancing with Catherine?

キャサリンと踊っているあいだ、ジョン・ソープはどんなことを話したでしょう。

Soon there was a pleasant surprise: Mr. Tilney arrived. He looked **dashing**. He was talking to a young lady who was very elegantly and fashionably dressed. Catherine guessed right away that the lady was his sister.

The two came walking near Catherine. He recognized her and smiled. She smiled back and they came over to her. He explained that he had left Bath for a week right after having met Catherine. He asked her for a dance, but Catherine did not accept because she had promised to dance with

John Thorpe, who, unexpectedly, returned this moment.

When Catherine started to dance with John, however, he did not **apologize** for having kept her waiting. And she was not pleased with the **conversation** during the dance. It was all about dogs and horses. ◆

02 Eleanor Tilney sits with Catherine

Answer the following questions in Japanese as you read the story.

1 What stopped Catherine from talking with Eleanor?
キャサリンはどうしてエレノアと話すのを止めたのでしょう。

2 What did Mrs. Thorpe say about her son?
ソープ夫人は自分の息子についてなんと言ったでしょう。

3 What was Henry Tilney doing while Catherine sat bored?
キャサリンが退屈して座っているとき、ヘンリー・ティルニーはどうしていたでしょう。

Catherine sat by herself after the dance. Soon Miss Tilney came to sit with her and introduced herself. Catherine was glad to know Eleanor Tilney. She was of a good figure and elegant **manners**. However, when they had hardly started to chat, Isabella interrupted them. She had come back with James. She sat on the other side of Catherine. "This is Mr. Tilney's sister," said Catherine softly. "What a lovely girl!" whispered Isabella. "Where's Mr. Tilney? Which one is he?" Isabella asked, but soon lost her interest because James asked her for another dance.

Then, Mrs. Allen and Mrs. Thorpe came to Catherine. Mrs. Thorpe asked, "Did you enjoy dancing with my son?" Catherine **politely** said, "Yes." The mother continued, "He really is a charming boy." Then Mrs. Allen said, "Did you see Mr. Tilney? He was here a little while ago. He wanted to dance with you." Catherine looked around for him and saw he was leading another young lady to dance. Mrs. Allen cried, "Oh, he has a partner now." Then Mrs. Thorpe said, "He certainly does. I am his mother, but I have to say he is the most charming young man in the world." Mrs. Allen whispered to Catherine, "I think she thought we were talking about her son." Then Catherine noticed that Eleanor had gone.

After this little **confusion**, John Thorpe himself came to Catherine and said, "Miss

Morland, get up. We have to dance again." Catherine said she was tired and he went away. For the rest of the evening Catherine sat bored: Isabella danced and talked with James, John Thorpe was gone, Eleanor was not to be seen, and Henry Tilney was dancing with his partner.

03 Riding out to the country

Answer the following questions in Japanese as you read the story.

1 Who came to pick up Catherine for a drive?
誰がキャサリンを迎えにきたでしょう。

2 Why was John Thorpe quiet on his carriage for some time?
ジョン・ソープは、どうして馬車でしばらく無口だったのでしょう。

3 About whom did John Thorpe ask questions of Catherine?
ジョン・ソープは誰についてキャサリンに尋ねましたか。

The following morning Catherine woke up feeling refreshed. She decided to make friends with Eleanor Tilney, who had left such a good impression.

At about noon, Mrs. Allen, looking out of the window, told Catherine that two carriages were outside. Catherine looked out and saw her brother James with Isabella in one, and John Thorpe was at the door. He cried to Catherine, "Hurry up, Miss Morland! The others are ready to go." "Where're you going?" "Don't say you have forgotten. We agreed to drive up to the country today." Catherine remembered she had heard something of that sort. But she was **doubtful** whether she had agreed to go.

"What do you think? Shall I go?" Catherine asked Mrs. Allen, who was not very helpful. "As you like, my dear," she said. Urged by the two faces in the carriage, Catherine went to her room to get ready and went down in a few minutes.

Isabella said, "It took you such a long time to get ready. We had a wonderful evening, didn't we? I have a lot to tell you about it. But now get in the carriage with John quickly." John said, giving her a hand, "My horse is a little wild at the beginning, but don't worry, Miss Morland. I'll **handle** him."

John Thorpe **concentrated** on handling his horse for a while and did not talk much. This calmed Catherine and she started to enjoy the scenery. Then suddenly, he asked her, "Old Mr. Allen is very rich, isn't he?"

Catherine was surprised at this unexpected question. "Ah, yes, I believe he is."

"No children?"

"No, I don't think he has any."

"And he is your **godfather**, right?"

"My godfather? No. He is our neighbour."

"But you are with him most of the time, aren't you?"

"Yes, I believe so."

"That's what I meant."

Catherine did not understand what he meant at all.

» Reviewing the story

I • Reorder a)~e) according to the story.

a) John and Isabella Thorpe and Catherine's brother James came to pick up Catherine for a ride to the country.

b) Catherine saw Henry Tilney dance with another girl.

c) Catherine had to refuse Henry Tilney, for she had promised to dance with John.

d) John Thorpe asked about Mr. Allen and his relationship with Catherine.

e) John Thorpe was quiet while concentrating on handling his horse.

II • Complete the sentences using the given words.

doubtful	confusion	godfather	politely	apologize

1 John did not [   ] to Catherine for having kept her waiting.

2 Eleanor was gone after a little [   ] caused by Isabella, Mrs. Allen and Mrs. Thorpe.

3 Catherine was [   ] if she had accepted John's invitation for a ride.

4 Catherine answered [   ] when Mrs. Thorpe asked if she had enjoyed dancing with John Thorpe.

5 John Thorpe tried to make sure that Mr. Allen was Catherine's "[   ]", and undoubtedly rich.

» Listening and oral practices

Fill the blanks as you listen and practice the conversation with your partner.

A : My horse is a little wild at the beginning. But don't worry. [1   ].

By the way, Mr. Allen is very rich, isn't he?

B : Mr. Allen? [2   ].

A : No children?

B : [3   ].

A：And he is your godfather, right?

B：My godfather? No. He is our neighbour.

A：[4   ], aren't you?

B：Yes, I believe so.

A：[5   ].

» Tips for reading

◀ 動名詞 ▶ は動詞を名詞成分に変え、主語、補語、動詞や前置詞の目的語にもなる。

Saying is one thing and **doing** is another.（主語）

Catherine is looking forward to **seeing** Henry again.（前置詞の目的語）

▶ 太字は現在分詞、動名詞のどちらでしょう。

1）John is **speeding** up his horse.

2）Catherine is not comfortable about John's aimless **speeding**.

3）John kept Catherine **waiting**.

4）It seems that Isabella does not mind **interrupting** people.

◀ 完了動名詞 ▶

形：having + 過去分詞

完了形の機能：本動詞との時間のずれ、あるいは行為や状態の完了や時間の幅を表す。

John kept Catherine waiting, but he did not apologize for it.

⇒ John did not apologize for **having kept Catherine waiting**.

▶ 動名詞を使って英語を完成しましょう。

1）Henry met Catherine but a week later he left Bath.

　　⇒ Henry left Bath a week after [   ].

2）Catherine accepted John as her dance partner, and then she probably blamed herself for it.

　　⇒ Catherine probably blamed herself of [   ] as her dance partner.

» Read a part of the original passage

Miss Tilney had a good figure, a pretty face, and a very agreeable countenance; and her air, though it had not all the decided pretension, the resolute stylishness of Miss Thorpe's, had more real elegance. Her manners showed good sense and good breeding; they were neither shy nor affectedly open; and she seemed capable of being young, attractive, and at a ball

without wanting to fix the attention of every man near her, and without exaggerated feelings of ecstatic delight or inconceivable vexation on every little trifling occurrence.

❯❯ Write a passage as a character

Write a passage of 3〜5 sentences from the diary of John Thorpe about the conversation with Catherine during the riding.

column 03　バースの賭博文化

　ジョン・ソープはキャサリンを残してカード・テーブルに行ってしまいましたね。それはギャンブルの場です。キャサリンと踊っているとき、ジョンがもっぱら馬や犬を語っていたことは、彼の競馬やドッグ・レースへの興味も示唆しています。競馬場は今もレースによっては社交の場となりますが、18 世紀にはロンドンやバースを始めイングランド各地で、カード・ギャンブルが男女や身分を問わず同等に勝負できる娯楽として受け入れられ、貴族の邸で行われるそうした場も社交の一環でした。

デヴォンシャー邸のギャンブル（中心はデヴォンシャー公爵夫人ジョージアナ）

　とはいえ上流が遊ぶときの賭け金は高く、一夜でひと財産負けてしまう人もありました。故ダイアナ元王妃の先祖の一人、美貌で知られたデヴォンシャー公爵夫人ジョージアナや劇作家で政治家のリチャード・シェリダンも、皇太子時代のジョージ四世といっしょに賭けトランプに興じており、シェリダンの代表作『悪口学校』（1777）には、カード・テーブルにつく登場人物それぞれの後ろに借金取りが待ちかまえている、といった描写があります。そうした遊興の中心地の一つが皇太子お気に入りの町バースだったのです。

　文学作品に登場する、ギャンブルで窮地に陥る上流の人物像を拾ってみましょう。スタンリー・キューブリック監督が映画化（1975 公開）したウィリアム・サッカレーの小説『バリー・リンドン（*The Luck of Barry Lyndon*）』（1844）の主役バリーはその一典型です。文豪ヘンリー・ジェイムズの遺作『抗議の叫び』（1911）では、貴族の長女が別の貴族女性にトランプで巨額の借金を作ってしまい、その穴埋めに次女が債権者の息子と結婚させられかけたり、代々伝わる名画が売却寸前となったりします。もう一例をあげると、マージョリー・ボーエンという女性作家の恐怖小説『地獄の司教』（1949）のエンディ

ングでは、賭け事などで身を持ち崩して地獄に落ちた上流出身の司教のおぞましい死に姿が読者に衝撃を与えます。

現実に戻ると、1768 年、バースの賭博室のカード・テーブルにおいて、シェリダンほどではないものの人気劇作家だったサミュエル・フートが、一晩で 1700 ポンド、今の価値で約 15 万ポンド負けたという記録が残っています。こうした悲劇が起きないよう、儀典長（キャサリンにヘンリーを正式に紹介した役どころ "the master of ceremonies"）の初代ボー・ナッシュ（本名リチャード・ナッシュ、1674-1761）は、賭博

ボー・ナッシュの肖像
©Michael Maggs

カード・ルームがあったバースの建物

室でいかさま師に目を光らせて、「カモ」になりかねない初心者に助言をしたり、また大金をすってしまった人を経済的に助けたりもしていました。賭博室やダンス会場やパンプ・ルームといったバースの社交場には一定の服装をして礼儀正しければ誰でも出入りできましたが、「刺繍生地の上衣を着ている人がすべて紳士だと思うのはまちがいだ」というナッシュの言葉が残っています。

しかしバースではカード・ルームのみならず「モーガン」や「オレンジ・グローヴ」といったコーヒー・ハウスでも盛んに賭けごとが行われるようになり、賭けの種類も増えていきました。地元刊行物には 1711 年の〈口笛競争〉や 1761 年の〈セダン・レース〉の主催が報告されています。

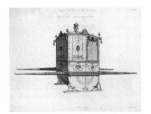

ロバート・アダムのデザインによるセダン・チェア（1775 年制作）

風紀の乱れについて政府は手をこまねいていたわけではありません。1711 年には〈ファロ〉や〈バセット〉と呼ばれる種類の賭けトランプを禁止し、1739 年にはより広範囲な賭け事取り締まり令を出しています。これはまさにバースを標的にした法律で、違反者には 20 ポンドの罰金を課してそれをバース病院への寄付としました。しかしバースで賭博が廃れることはなく、アッセンブリー・ルームに付属する賭博室オクタゴン・ルームが手狭になると 1777 年、あらたにカード・ルームを増設したのです。小説中でジョン・ソープがいそいそと出向いたのはこの部屋ですね。

なにしろ国のトップである摂政皇太子（後のジョージ 4 世）がバースの賭博文化を率先していたのですから取り締まりが行き届くはずはなく、1800 年代に入ってもバースでは上流がまるで「名声」を競うかのように大金をはって賭けごとを続けていました。これがようやく下火になったのは中層道徳の体現をイメージ戦略としたヴィクトリア女王の治世になってからで、1845 年と 1853 年の賭博を取り締まる法律が効を発したと言われます。このころには徐々に社会の論調も、ギャンブルを反道徳的な堕落した娯楽と見るようになっていきました。

とは言えヴィクトリア時代には、今度は貧しい暮らしや辛い労働の憂さ晴らしを求める下層が、都市の道端でさまざまな賭けに興じる姿が目立つようになり、一方、人目を避けた会員制クラブの形をとる富裕層向けの賭博場もそこここで営業していました。バースでは、ブライドウェル横丁やスノウ・ヒルで、また大掛かりなものとしては 1897 年、ストール通り 23 番地 A 号やクィーン・スクエアの「バース・アンド・カントリー・クラブ」で賭博行為が検挙されています。さらに 1911 年、アッパー・バラ・ウォールで表向きはレストランを経営していたエレン・ガストンという女性の元締めが検挙・連行された記録があります。

こうして一時地下に潜ったバースの賭博文化ですが、結局は絶えることなく、1963年に「モナコ・ルーム」が認可カジノとして営業を始めると庶民にも人気を博し、経営者ジョン・リチャードソンとヴィート・チェンタモアは一晩中営業する許可を得てキャバレーを併設します。これは大いに繁盛し、この後にジョージ通りの「ヘイドリアン・クラブ」などが続きました。

さて、今はバースを訪れるとあっけらかんと昼間に営業しているカジノで家族づれや観光客が楽しく少額のかけ金で遊んでいるのに出くわします。ホテルのスタッフから「カジノはバースに安定雇用を生み出してきた」と聞くと、ジェインの時代に育まれた「社交と遊興」の文化は長い目で見るとこの町を成長させたのだ、とも感じます。

バースのセンチュリー・カジノ
（チェーン店）

参考資料

"History of Gaming in Bath" *Bath Magazine*
https://thebathmagazine.co.uk/history-house-cards/ 2021 6/19 取得
"Coffee Houses" in *Bath Past*
http://www.buildinghistory.org/bath/georgian/coffeehouses.shtml 2021 6/19 取得

≫ Get ready with vocabulary!

Match the Japanese words 1～10 with the English words given below.

1 遠出   2 探るように   3 注意を払って   4 結婚持参金
5 面白がっている   6 恥をかかせる
7 ちゃんとした   8 例える   9 素朴で無知な
10 熱心に・じぃっと

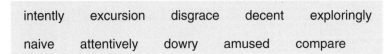

| intently | excursion | disgrace | decent | exploringly |
| naive | attentively | dowry | amused | compare |

≫ Enjoy the story!

01 About the Tilney family

Answer the following questions in Japanese as you read the story.

1 In the Pump Room, who did Mrs. Allen talk with?
アレン夫人はパンプ・ルーム（鉱泉を飲むための社交広間）で誰と話をしたでしょう。

2 What do you know about Henry Tilney now?
ヘンリー・ティルニーについて何がわかりましたか。

3 What do you know about late Mrs. Tilney?
亡くなったティルニー夫人について何がわかりましたか。

(1-14)

Catherine came back to Allen's lodging at about three in the afternoon.

"How was your **excursion**?" asked Mrs. Allen.

"Very nice, thank you. Did you have a good day?" asked Catherine.

"Yes, I went to the Pump Room today. I saw Mrs. Thorpe there. She was glad that you went out with her son today."

"Who else did you see?" Catherine asked rather **exploringly**.

"I saw Mr. and Miss Tilney. I talked with them for quite some time and learned a lot about them. Mr. Tilney is a clergyman. I think they are good people and very well off. They come from Gloucestershire."

Now Catherine was listening very **attentively**. "Yes? Which part of Gloucestershire?"

"I asked, but I forgot. Anyway, their mother, Mrs. Tilney, was Miss Drummond

before her marriage. Her father gave her twenty thousand pounds as a **dowry** and five hundred pounds for her wedding clothes. Of course, this was not the topic we talked about with Mr. and Miss Tilney." ◆

"Does Mrs. Tilney live in Gloucester with her husband?"

"Yes, ... oh, no. She died quite a while ago, umm, if I remember Miss Tilney's words correctly."

"And the young Mr. Tilney, is he the only son?"

"I'm not sure, Catherine."

Catherine felt that she had learned all she could from Mrs. Allen.

02 A conversation with Eleanor Tilney

Answer the following questions in Japanese as you read the story.

1 Why did Catherine feel left out?

どうしてキャサリンは、仲間外れになっていると感じたのでしょう。

2 What made Eleanor look amused?

エレノアは何を面白がったのでしょう。

3 What was Eleanor aware of?

エレノアは何に気づいていたでしょう。

The next day, Catherine went to the Pump Room as usual. She met up with Isabella and James, who were now constantly together. They were whispering to each other and Catherine felt left out. Then she saw Miss Tilney coming into the room and gladly went to talk with her.

Nothing very important was said by either, but the conversation was pleasant. Eleanor too seemed to be pleased to talk with Catherine.

"Your brother dances very well," Catherine said.

"Who? Henry?" Eleanor looked **amused**.

"I am very sorry I couldn't dance with him last time because I had already agreed to dance with Mr. Thorpe. The young lady who danced with your brother, was she Miss Smith?"

"That's right."

"I'm sure your brother was pleased. Do you think she is pretty?"

"Not very," answered Eleanor. Now she looked more amused.

"Is your brother coming to the Pump Room today?"

"No. Today he has gone out with our father."

"Will you be at the dance tomorrow?"

"Perhaps, if we…. Yes! Definitely, we'll be there." Eleanor said good-bye and left the Pump Room. Catherine went home with a lighter heart. Now all she had to decide was what to wear tomorrow night.

Maybe Catherine was not aware herself, but as you have rightly guessed, Eleanor was clearly aware of Catherine's feeling towards her brother Henry.

03 Henry Tilney reveals his feelings

Answer the following questions in Japanese as you read the story.

1 Who was standing in front of Catherine?

誰がキャサリンの前に立っていましたか。

2 How did John Thorpe lie to Catherine?

ジョン・ソープはキャサリンにどんな嘘をつきましたか。

3 What do marriage and dance have in common, according to Henry Tilney?

ヘンリー・ティルニーは、結婚とダンスにはどんな共通点があると言っていますか。 1-16

Next evening, Catherine, trying her best to avoid John Thorpe, looked for Henry. She hoped Henry would ask her to dance for the third time. The first part of the evening had passed without her catching the sight of his figure. Catherine had begun to feel it was silly to hope to find him in that crowded room even if he was there. Then she noticed someone was standing in front of her. It was Henry Tilney himself. He asked her to dance and she answered "Yes".

They were about to begin their first dance of that evening, when John Thorpe came over to them and took Catherine a few metres apart from Henry.

"What are you doing, Miss Morland? I thought you were going to dance with me."

"You never asked me," replied Catherine.

"I asked you as soon as I came here, remember? I've been telling everyone that I am going to dance with the prettiest girl in the room tonight. So, if you dance with someone else, you'll **disgrace** me."

"Oh, then there is no problem. No one will identify me with that description."

"Who are you dancing with, anyway?" He looked at Henry and said, "Oh, Tilney. He is a **decent** man. Does he want a horse? Ask him if he wants a horse. I have a friend who wants to sell a good horse."

Catherine left John talking and hurried back to Henry.

Now Henry Tilney had something to say to Catherine.

"I was getting angry with the gentleman," said Henry as soon as Catherine joined him. "You have accepted to dance with me for this evening. It was rude of him to take your attention from me in that way. I think of dance as being like a marriage."

"How?" Catherine could not help asking. "If a man and a woman get married, they cannot be separated. But when they dance, they only stand opposite each other in the ball room for half an hour or so," said Catherine.

Henry was ready to answer. "So, you think marriage and dance can't be **compared**. Then let me explain. In both, the man has the advantage of choice. The woman can only accept or reject. In both, arrangements are made for advantage of both a man and a woman. They belong to each other. That's their duty. Both must not try to give an excuse or reason to be with someone else. Don't you agree?"

If Catherine was **naive**, she was honest, too. "Yes, I agree. But I still think dance and marriage are quite different things."

"Then, your sense of duty to your dancing partner is not as strict as your partner wishes. Do you think if the gentleman comes up to you now, you can talk with him if you want to?"

"He is a close friend of my brother's. I have no choice but to talk with him. But I don't want to talk with anybody now. I want to dance with you."

"Ah, I'm now satisfied." Henry smiled. Then he continued as gently as before. "Are you enjoying Bath?" The music started and Catherine answered, "Yes, more and more." They concentrated on the dance.

At this point, Catherine did not know that an older gentleman among the onlookers was **intently** watching her.

❯❯ Reviewing the story

I ● Reorder a)～e) according to the story.

a) Catherine felt left out because James and Isabella whispered each other.

b) Henry Tilney made a little speech about marriage and dance.

c) When Henry Tilney and Catherine were about to dance, John Thorpe interrupted them.

d) Catherine drew some information on the Tilney family from Mrs. Allen.

e) Catherine had a pleasant little talk with Eleanor Tilney.

II • Complete the sentences using the given words.

| amused | intently | compared | identify | dowry |

1 Mrs. Tilney brought a big [   ] to General Tilney.

2 The conversation with Catherine [   ] Eleanor very much.

3 Catherine talked back to John Thorpe that people would not [   ] her with his description of "the prettiest girl in the room".

4 Catherine was not convinced at all when Henry Tilney [   ] marriage to dance.

5 An older gentleman among the onlookers was looking at Catherine [   ].

» Listening and oral practices

Fill the blanks as you listen and practice the conversation with your partner. (1-17)

A：What are you doing, Miss Morland? I thought [¹   ].

B：You never asked me.

A：[²   ], remember? I've been telling everyone that I am
going to dance with the prettiest girl in this room. So, if you dance with someone else,
[³   ].

A：Oh, then there is no problem. [⁴   ].

» Tips for reading

◀ It takes 人 + 時間 / 労力 / 活動　to-verb ▶ = 人が to-verb するのに時間 / 労力 / 活動が要る。

"**It took you such a long time to get ready,**" said Isabella.（Chapter 3）

▶ 英語を完成しましょう。

アレン夫人からティルニー家の情報を得るのにキャサリンは辛抱強い（patient）会話をしなく
てはいけなかった。

It took [   ] some information on the Tilneys from Mrs. Allen.

◀ 動名詞の主語 ▶

The first part of the evening had passed without **her catching** the sight of his figure.

すでにその夜の初めのほうは、彼女が彼の姿を目にすることなく過ぎていました。

John sped up his horse in spite of **Catherine asking** to halt it.

キャサリンが停めてと頼んだのにジョンは馬のスピードをあげた。

▶ 主語を伴う動名詞を使って英語を完成しましょう。

29

キャサリンは了承して（agree/consent）いなかったのに、ジョン・ソープは彼女に自分と踊るよう促した。

John Thorpe urged Catherine to dance with him without [   ] to do so.

◆ 名詞節を導く **if** ◆ （= whether）

Ask him **if** (= **whether**) **he wants a horse** (**or not**). 馬が欲しいかどうか、彼に聞いてくれよ。

▶ 英語を完成しましょう。

A：I wonder [   ]. キャサリンはジョンが好きなのかしら。

B：She is probably grumbling to him in her mind, "Don't even ask me [   ]!"
　　おそらく心中で「一緒に踊りたいかなんて尋ねられるのも嫌だわ」って呟いているよ。

◆ 同格の **that** ◆「～という」

Henry gave Catherine his idea **that** a man has the advantage of choice both in marriage and in dance.

ヘンリーは、結婚とダンスの両方において男性が選択の優先権を持つという考えをキャサリンに述べました。

▶ 英語を完成しましょう。

This time Catherine was not flattered with [   ]
in the room.

今回キャサリンは、部屋にいるなかで彼女が一番きれいな女の子だというジョンの描写でいい気分になったりしませんでした。

　参考）指示語や代名詞以外の that の機能に気をつけましょう。以下はその一部です。

① Henry thinks **that** men have advantage in choosing their dance partner.（名詞節を導く）

② Catherine does not entirely accept the idea about dance and marriage **that** Henry gave to her.（関係代名詞）

③ Henry was glad **that** Catherine wanted to dance with him.（～して嬉しい）
　 John is rude **that** he drives Catherine into dancing with him.（～するとは失礼だ）
　 （形容詞・自動詞などに続く節を導き、理由や判断の基準を表す）

④ John was so rude **that** he tried to push Catherine to dance with him.（so～を受ける）

◆ 前置詞 **but** ◆　「～以外に」

I have no choice **but** to talk with him.

話さないわけにいかないわ。（話す以外に選択肢はない。）

▶ 前置詞 **but** を使って書き換えましょう。

Eleanor could not help noticing Catherine's feeling towards Henry.

⇒ Eleanor [   ] towards Henry.

I think I could place them in such a view. You will allow, that in both, man has the advantage of choice, woman only the power of refusal; that in both, it is an engagement between man and woman, formed for the advantage of each; and that when once entered into, they belong exclusively to each other till the moment of its dissolution; that it is their duty, each to endeavour to give the other no cause for wishing that he or she had bestowed themselves elsewhere, and their best interest to keep their own imaginations from wandering towards the perfections of their neighbours, or fancying that they should have been better off with anyone else.

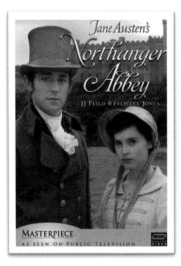

» Write a passage as a character

Write a passage of 3〜5 sentences from the diary of Henry Tilney about the conversation he had with Catherine just before dancing with her.

---

column 04

ダンスの流行

　ジェイン・オースティンの小説におけるダンスについて、ナンシー・M・リー＝リフェという研究者は３つの機能を挙げています。まずダンスという場を設定することで、他の場所では出会うことのなさそうなさまざまな登場人物たちを出会わせて、伏線を仕込んだり人間関係を発展させたりして巧妙に物語を前に進めている。次にダンスをしながらの気構えのない会話によって人物像を鮮やかに描いている。そして、じっさいにダンスを楽しんでいた当時の読者になじみのある場面を描くことで、虚構の世界をアットホームに感じさせた、というものです。最初の二点は、本書でキャサリンとジョンとヘンリーの三者によるダンス場での絡みを読まれた皆さんには納得の指摘でしょう。

　三つ目の、当時の読者がダンスになじんでいたという点ですが、18世紀後半徐々に広まり始めたダンスは、まさに1790年代から1810年代に急激に普及し、田舎は田舎の、都会は都会の社交にかかせないものとなっていました。本書巻末の「作者ジェイン・オースティンについて」でも触れますが、ジェイン自身も地元の名家が主宰するダンス・パーティに出かけて恋のお相手に出会ったようです。

　この時期、ダンス音楽やステップの解説や踊るときのエチケットなどを指南する出版物が次々と出され、人々はそれらを参考にして複雑な男女の動きの練習を積んでから、いざダン

ジェイン・オースティンの時代のダンスの5つの基本ポジション

ス会場へと向かいました。当時、少なくとも200種類以上のステップと動線があったことが確認されています。名称と動きの一致や流行は地方や時期によってしばらく流動的でしたが、「リール」「ジグ」「ハンブルグワルツ」など、イングランド中でほぼ一斉に大流行したステップもありました。ダンスの研究書も出版され、王立オペラ劇場（通称オペラハウス）のダンスマスターの地位にあったトマス・ウィルソンが1808年に初版を出した *The Analysis of Country Dancing* が最初の体系的なダンスの考察とされます。この著書の後の版によると、イングランドの社交ダンスは1815年ごろ、形と名称が定まって完成を見たということです。ま

パンプ・ルームのエッチング（19世紀中ごろ）

さにジェインの人生は、イギリスにおける社交ダンスの普及と完成の時期に重なっていたのですね。

参考資料

Nancy M. Lee-Riffe "The role of the country dance in the fiction of Jane Austen" *Women's* Writing, Volume 5, 1998 - Issue 1（Published Online: 19 Dec 2006）
https://www.tandfonline.com/doi/abs/10.1080/09699089800200032 2020年10月1日取得
"Dance through history-Regency Dance"（author unknown）
http://www.earlydancecircle.co.uk/resources/dance-through-history/regency-dance/ 2020年9月8日取得
"Regency dance" (author unknown)
https://www.regencydances.org/　2020年10月1日取得

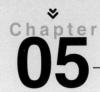

Chapter

05

NORTHANGER ABBEY

» Get ready with vocabulary!

Match the Japanese words 1～10 with the English words given below.

1 厳しい　　 2 ひと目を気にしている　　 3 不都合である

4 迷っている　　 5 確信したようすで　　 6 無視する

7 怒り心頭である　　 8 慰める　　 9 必死で　　 10 表情

ignore	comfort	desperately	inconvenient	stern
hesitant	assuredly	furious	self-conscious	expression

» Enjoy the story!

01　General Tilney

Answer the following questions in Japanese as you read the story.

1 Why did Catherine become self-conscious?

キャサリンはどうして人目が気になりだしたのでしょう。

2 Who was the older gentleman watching Catherine?

キャサリンを見ている年配の紳士は誰だったでしょう。

3 What did Eleanor Tilney invite Catherine to do?

エレノア・ティルニーはキャサリンを何に誘いましたか。

When the music stopped, Catherine noticed an older gentleman watching her. He looked rather **stern** but handsome as well. Then Henry excused himself and went to talk with him. The gentleman was still looking at Catherine while they were talking. She became very **self-conscious** and felt a little uneasy. Henry came back and said to her, "The gentleman was asking your name. So, you have the right to know his. He is General Tilney, my father." Catherine said, "Oh," with a great interest.

That evening, she had another opportunity to chat with Eleanor Tilney. They talked about the beautiful scenery of the country around Bath. Eleanor invited Catherine to walk with her brother and herself the next day. "I'll call for you at twelve o'clock tomorrow, if it is not **inconvenient**." Catherine gladly agreed. ◆

She wanted to tell Isabella what happened that evening, but Isabella was not to be seen anywhere in the room.

02 Missing each other

Answer the following questions in Japanese as you read the story.

1 Apart from the cloudy sky and the fact that Henry and Eleanor were late for the appointment, what enticed Catherine to go with John Thorpe?

曇り空やヘンリーとエレノアが約束に遅れていたこととは別に、キャサリンがジョン・ソープと出かけようと思った理由は何だったでしょう。

2 How did John Thorpe react to Catherine's pleading to stop his carriage?

キャサリンが馬車を止めるよう頼んだとき、ジョン・ソープはどう反応しましたか。

3 Why could not Catherine reach Blaise Castle?

キャサリンはなぜブレイズ城まで行けなかったのでしょう。

It was grey and dull the next morning. Catherine watched the sky from the window worrying about the weather. Unfortunately, at about eleven o'clock it started to rain.

Answer attentions to the weather.

"Probably no walk today." Catherine sighed. At about a half past noon, however, the sky began to clear the clouds and the sun came out. "Perhaps Henry and Eleanor will come here soon."

Seeing off Mr. and Mrs. Allen going to the Pump Room from the window, Catherine noticed two carriages coming along at a high speed. Once again, it was John and Isabella Thorpe with James.

"Hurry up! We're going to Bristol!" John called to her.

"Bristol? Oh, no. Today I can't go. I'm expecting some friends of mine. They might come at any moment."

"We go to Bristol and Blaise Castle*."

"Blaise Castle!"

"The finest and oldest castle with some towers just like the ones that appear in the novel you're reading."

Now Catherine was **hesitant**. "I'd like to see the castle but…. No. I can't. I'm expecting Mr. and Miss Tilney."

"They won't come. On our way to come here, we saw them on the carriage going out of Bath." John said **assuredly**. Catherine was surprised and very disappointed.

She thus decided to have a look at the old castle. Though she was not entirely happy, she started off to Bristol on John's carriage. As the four of them travelled out of Bath, however, their carriages passed Henry and Eleanor. They were walking towards Allen's lodging.

"Stop! Stop! Stop!" cried Catherine. "Let me get off and talk to them!" Henry and Eleanor seemed to have noticed her, but John **ignored** her cry and whipped his horse. "Why did you tell me a lie? How could you do this to me?" Catherine was now **furious**.

John Thorpe said that he had made a mistake. However, he did not stop his carriage nor apologize. Catherine tried to **comfort** herself with the thought that she should soon see the famous castle. But then, after some time, it became evident that they had left too late to go all the way to the castle as well as to Bristol. Besides, it started to rain again. Since John's carriage had no ceiling, Catherine almost ruined her gown.

When Catherine reached back her lodging, the maid told her that Henry and Eleanor Tilney had come for her a few minutes after she had left. Catherine felt so frustrated and unhappy that she could not fall asleep for a long time that night.

* Blaise Castle ブレイズ城は、要塞や居城として建てられた本来の城ではなく、主に 18 世紀にイギリスの金持ちが領地の森や庭園に装飾用に作った "folly" と総称される建築物の一つ。それらはしばしば古代建築や中世の古城風にしたてられた。

03 At the theatre

Answer the following questions in Japanese as you read the story.

1 What made Henry Tilney smile again?

ヘンリー・ティルニーはどうして、再び微笑んだのでしょう。

2 What made Catherine feel flattered at the theatre?

劇場でキャサリンが気分よくなったのはなぜでしょう。

3 What did Isabella's letter say?

イザベラの手紙には何が書かれていましたか。

The following night, the Allens and Catherine went to the theatre. Since the Tilneys were not to be seen, Catherine tried to concentrate on the play. Just as she was beginning to enjoy the performance, she saw General Tilney and Henry joining the audience opposite her box seat. Henry noticed and looked at her, but his **expression** was not so friendly. The first part of the play finally ended. Catherine noticed

Henry had left his seat. Catherine **desperately** hoped that he would be coming to her booth to say hello.

Soon he showed himself and greeted Mr. and Mrs. Allen and Catherine very politely. Catherine could not hold herself another moment. "Oh! My apologies, Mr. Tilney. It wasn't my fault. They told me that you and your sister had gone out of Bath in a carriage. Then I saw you two were walking. I would much rather have been with you!"

Henry smiled. "You didn't stop your carriage to wish us a pleasant walk." He said this jokingly, but Catherine was serious. "I tried, but Mr. Thorpe didn't stop. I wanted to jump off and run after you." This made Henry smile again. In fact, he almost laughed. Then he went out of her booth.

Then Catherine noticed that General Tilney was talking with John Thorpe. John soon came to her. She asked, "How did you come to know him? He is General Tilney, isn't he?"

"I was in the Navy, so I know a lot of people," proudly said John. "The General was asking about you. He thinks you are the finest girl in Bath and I totally agreed with him."

Catherine was very much flattered with the General's comment and left the theatre feeling happiest that night.

John Thorpe came to take Catherine for a ride a few times during the next week, but Catherine did not want to upset the Tilneys, so she did not go with him. Instead, she was invited to dinner at Tilney's and was looking forward to it.

Then one day, Catherine received a message from Isabella. It said:

Dearest Catherine,
I have a very important news. I cannot write it down in a letter.
I need to see you.

Love, Isabella

❯❯ Reviewing the story

Ⅰ ● Reorder a) ～e) according to the story.

a) Catherine joined John, Isabella and James to ride out to the country.

b) The older gentleman staring at Catherine turned out to be Henry Tilney's father.

c) Catherine saw John Thorpe talking with General Tilney.

d) Eleanor Tilney invited Catherine to take a walk together with her brother Henry and herself.

e) Eleanor and Henry Tilney might have noticed Catherine on John's carriage while they were walking to Catherine's lodging.

II ● Complete the sentences using the given words.

self-conscious	ignored	desperately	stern	hesitant

1 The older gentleman who talked with Henry Tilney looked [   ].
2 Noticing someone was watching her, Catherine became [   ].
3 Catherine was [   ] about going on a ride at the beginning.
4 John Thorpe [   ] Catherine's cry to stop the carriage.
5 Catherine [   ] hoped to have a chance to apologize to Henry Tilney.

» Listening and oral practices

Fill the blanks as you listen and practice the conversation with your partner.

A : [¹   ]! We are going to Bristol!

B : Bristol? Oh, no! I can't go. I'm expecting some friends. [²   ]

A : We go to Blaise Castle!

B : Blaise Castle!

A : The castle with some towers, just like [³   ] you're reading.

B : I'd like to see Blaise Castle but⋯. No, I can't. I'm expecting Mr. and Miss Tilney.

A : They won't come. [⁴   ], we saw them on the carriage going out of Bath.

» Tips for reading

◀ 先行詞を含む関係代名詞 what ▶ 「～のところのもの / こと（すべて）」

Catherine wanted to tell Isabella **what happened that evening.**
キャサリンはイザベラに**その夜起こったことを**言いたかった。（「その夜何が起こったのか」と、what が導く名詞節ととらえてもよい。）

Catherine felt that she had learned **what** (= **all / all that**) **she could** from Mrs. Allen. (Chapter 4)
キャサリンは、アレン夫人から聞き出せることは全て聞き出した、と感じた。

"You are **what you wear**."—Coco Chanel.
着ているものすなわちあなたよ。—ココ・シャネル

▶ 英語を完成しましょう。

1) Maybe Catherine should know that [   ] makes a part of her mind.
   キャサリンには、読んでいるものは心の一部となる、と知ってほしいものです。

2）Mr. and Mrs. Morland were doing [   ] to raise their ten children.　モーランド夫妻は 10 人の子を育てるためできるだけのことをしていた。

be 動詞 + to 不定詞　　が可能・能力・予定・義務・運命・意図などを表す場合。

Isabella **was not to be seen** anywhere in the room. イザベラの姿はどこにも見えなかった。

Catherine **was to leave** Bath without the Allens.（Chapter 7）

キャサリンはアレン夫妻と離れてバースを去ることになったのでした。（Chapter 7）

Catherine and Henry missed each other and John **was to blame** for that.

キャサリンとヘンリーは会い損ね、そのことで責められるべきはジョンだった。

▶ **be + to〜 を使って英語を完成しましょう。**

1）Since the Tilneys [   ], Catherine tried to concentrate on the play.

ティルニー家の人々が見えなかったのでキャサリンは劇に集中しようとしました。

2）Soon Catherine [   ] an important news from Isabella.

まもなくキャサリンはイザベラから重要な知らせを聞くことになります。

3）Catherine [   ] "No" to the invitation for the excursion; Blaise Castle was too exciting to miss.

キャサリンは遠出の誘いを断れませんでした。ブレイズ城は、見逃すにはあまりにワクワクするものでしたから。

🔹 Read a part of the original passage

Catherine looked round and saw Miss Tilney leaning on her brother's arm, walking slowly

Laura Place, Bath

down the street. She saw them both looking back at her. "Stop, stop, Mr. Thorpe," she impatiently cried; "it is Miss Tilney; it is indeed. How could you tell me they were gone? Stop, stop, I will get out this moment and go to them." But to what purpose did she speak? Thorpe only lashed his horse into a brisker trot; the Tilneys, who had soon ceased to look after

her, were in a moment out of sight around the corner of Laura Place, and in another moment, she was herself whisked into the marketplace.

🔹 Write a passage as a character

Write a passage of 3〜6 sentences from Catherine's diary about what happened at the theatre.

イングランド劇場事情

column
05 **イングランド劇場事情**

『ノーサンガー・アビー』を読むと劇場が社交の場であることがうかがえますね。観客たちが着飾った姿をお互いに披露する場であることは一七世紀から変っていないようです。

イングランドにおける最初の劇場黄金期は言うまでもなくウィリアム・シェイクスピア（1564-1616）、そしてジョン・ウェブスター（c.1578-c.1626）やベン・ジョンソン（c.1572-c.1637）らが活躍した時代です。シェイクスピアに代表される時代の劇場は、主に古代ローマの屋外半円形劇場の流れを汲む円形劇場でした。それを今のような屋内の、舞台と向かい合う客席にして定着させたのは、建築家イニゴー・ジョーンズ（1573-1652）とその後援者である王妃ヘンリエッタ＝マリア（1609-1669）です。王妃の母はイタリアのメディチ家からフランスのブルボン家に嫁いだマリー・ド・メディシス（1575-1642）で、娘の輿入れ行事で展示すべく、連作《マリー・ド・メディシスの生涯》をペーテル・ルーベンスに描かせ、芸術の威力を実感させて娘をイングランド王チャールズ一世（1600-1649）のもとへ送り出しました。この連作は今もルーブル美術館で見学者を圧倒しています。このところヘンリエッタ・マリアのチャールズへの影響の大きさが見直されていますが、イニゴー・ジョーンズの劇場は、フランス、ブルボン家のルイ一四世に倣って、イングランドの王と側近たちが自ら舞台に上がり、限られた人々を招いて手の込んだ舞台美術と王の優雅な動きを披露する場へと変化しました。

チャールズ一世が処刑されて清教徒時代になると劇場はいったん閉鎖されます。しかし続

く王政復古期（1660-1688）には厳格な前の時代への反動からか娯楽全般が盛んになりました。とはいえ劇場は基本的に王の認可を得た数カ所に絞られていました。なぜなら劇場は、現代の欧州や南米のサッカー場のように暴動を警戒すべき場所だったので、数を限定して監視下に置く必要があったからです。シェイクスピアの時代には変声期以前の少年が女性を演じていましたが、この王制復古期に「女優」が登場しました。彼女たちの多くに貴族の後援者がついており、なかにはネル・グウィン（1650-1687）のように、劇場のオレンジ水の売り子から女優に、ついには王の側室となって息子に爵位を賜る人まで現れました。

《ネル・グイン》(c.1675)
ピーター・レリー作（モデルについては再検討の動きもある）

一八世紀になると劇場はその数は増やし、そこは金持ちにとっては余分にいくらか払って舞台に座り、衣装や髪型を見せびらかす場となりました。彼らは、例えば大ヒット作『乞食オペラ』（1728）出演のラヴィニア・フェントン（1706-1760）という人気女優が演じている舞台へ、料金（チップ）を払って上がりこみ、彼女を近くで眺めたり、ときに上演中に口説いたり、また演技に合いの手を入れたりしていたのです。役者が動けないほど大勢の客が舞台にあがってしまうこともありました。

これをなくしたのが名優デヴィッド・ギャリック（1717-1779）です。客を客席にとどめ、役柄に合う鬘や衣装を用意し、大仰な演技をやめました。複雑な心理表現に長け、シェイクスピア作品にリアリズムを吹き込んだとされます。ハムレットの父の

《ディヴィッド・ギャリック》
(1770) トマス・ゲインズバラ作

幽霊役では、客を震撼させると同時に涙させました。無認可劇場で演じたリチャード三世役が注目され、1741年、ドルリーレーン劇場に移り、5年後には監督とプロデューサーと劇場支配人を兼ねる「マネージャー」に就任しました。1682年からのロングラン作品にT・オトウェイ作『守られたベニス』がありますが、これは親友に誘われてベニス政府転覆を謀る男が妻の説得によって思いとどまり、逆に親友をナイフで刺したあと自死するという悲劇です。単純なストーリーながら、ギャリックが演じる主役は「声の調子やポーズの多彩さは驚嘆に値する」と評されました。

そしてジェイン・オースティンの時代、世紀の変わり目を挟んで劇場シーンを席巻したのは、旅役者の一座を主宰する両親のもとに生まれたケンブル姉弟でした。弟ジョンは1780年代前半、ドルリーレーン劇場でのハムレット役や、姉のサラ・シドンズ（形だけ夫のシドンズ姓を名乗った）とともに演じた『マクベス』で注目され、後には妹や弟も俳優として大きな名声を得ています。サラとジョンが共演する悲劇は「電撃が走る」とまで評されました。ジョンは1788年ドルリーレーンのマネージャーとなりましたが、1803年にコヴェントガーデン劇場の株の6分の1を入

《シドンズ夫人》（1785）トマス・ゲインズバラ作

シェリダンの代表作の一つ『恋がたき』のバース巡業のチラシ ©Bodleian Libraries
主演のファニー・ケンブルがシドンズ夫人の妹であると言及されている

手してからは、入場料値上げをめぐる観客たちの暴動や劇場運営の苦労が続きました。一方、姉のサラは、重鎮ギャリックの演出が肌に合わず、その影響を逃れて一時バースに拠点をおき、バースの演劇界を牽引しました。しかし1779年にギャリックが死ぬとロンドンに戻り、「悲劇の女王」としてイギリス演劇界の大黒柱となりました。サラは、演劇人である親族の協力と自らの実力によって、パトロンを持たずに芸能のみで生計をたて子どもまで育てた初の本格的職業女優となりました。

さてジェイン・オースティンの時代、

《リンリー姉妹》（c.1772）（部分、エリザ） トマス・ゲインズバラ作

舞台は多様化を迎えていました。このころの芸能関係者で特筆すべきは、1770年代から活躍した劇作家パーシー・B・シェリダン（1751-1816）と、その妻で「元祖アイドル歌手」のエリザベス・リンリー（1754-1799）、通称エリザです。エリザの本拠地はバースでした。彼女の実家はバースで当時注目のおしゃれな集合住宅ロイヤル・クレッセントにあり、そこで音楽家の父が催すサークルが彼女の出発点でした。野

バースのロイヤル・クレッセント

心家の父は体面のためにロイヤル・クレッセントに居を構

シェリダンと摂政皇太子とその恋人フィッツハーバート夫人の企みを風刺するエッチング（1791）©National Portrait Gallery

えて音楽会やレッスンで収入を得る一方、エリザを 13 歳のときからバースの街角で歌わせてチップを集めさせていました。16, 7 歳になったエリザが歌うバース大聖堂や教会には遠くからも人が押し寄せ、ストーカーまがいの「おっかけ」たちまで現れました。

　シェリダンは最初その一人でしたが、ことに執拗なストーカーから彼女を守るというポーズで強引にエリザと駆け落ちし、既成事実を作って妻にしました。ところが結婚後は女優たちと浮名を流し、しかも自ら招いた数度の破産や決闘を、人気と人望の厚かったエリザの援助やとりなしによって免れるような男でした。しかもついには皇太子の派閥の国会議員となり、派手で巧みな国会演説によって注目もされました。

　しかしシェリダンの業績はやはり政治でなく劇作にあります。上流の機知に富む会話で進む風習劇を確立し、日常の人間関係を描いて新たな境地を開きました。この分野は一世紀のちオスカー・ワイルド（1854-1900）が精錬することになります。2000 年のある統計によると、イギリスでシェイクスピアの次に上演回数が多い脚本家はシェリダンでした。

　いま少しジェインのころの劇場を追ってみましょう。続く時代のスターは、４才から舞台に立ったエドマンド・キーン（1787-1833）でした。ドルリーレーン劇場の 3000 席を一杯にできる数少ない俳優の一人で、「死」の演技が卓越していました。1814 年、『ベニスの商人』のシャイロック役では、幕開けから最後まで拍手の渦が続いたと記録されます。しかし私生活は奇行と醜聞に満ち、ある人妻との姦通罪で告訴されたあとは、ロンドンとニューヨークでヤジと罵倒を受けて上演の中断を余儀なくされます。1833 年『オセロ』で息子と共演したあととうとう引退を決め、２カ月後、46 才で他界しました。キーンの、シェリダンの人生と並ぶ「劇的」人生は、サルトルやデュマの作品の題材となりました。

参考資料：
『イギリスを知るための 65 章』近藤久雄他著 62-63 章（明石書店 2014 年）
"The 18th century theatre" in *The History of English Theatre* by David Timson（2021; Kindle Book）
他

Chapter 06

» Get ready with vocabulary!

Match the Japanese words 1~10 with the English words given below.

1 承諾　　2 うなずく　　3 はらはらしている状態

4 賞賛する　　5 非難する　　6 誉め言葉　　7 仰天させる

8 （肩を）すぼめる　　9 話題　　10 気前がいい

admire	astonish	shrug	blame	consent
compliment	subject	generous	nod	suspension

» Enjoy the story!

01 An engagement

Answer the following questions in Japanese as you read the story.

1 What news did Isabella Thorpe bring to Catherine?

イザベラ・ソープはどんな知らせをキャサリンにもたらしましたか。

2 What was John Thorpe satisfied with?

ジョン・ソープは何に満足したのですか。

3 What was Catherine worried about?

キャサリンは何を心配していましたか。

2-1

"Oh, Catherine! Your brother is a wonderful person. I'm so happy!"

"What happened?" asked Catherine. Isabella said, "I only wish I will meet his expectation as his wife." Catherine slowly began to understand what her news was. "Yes, Catherine. James proposed to me and I've accepted his proposal. He is on his way to Fullerton to ask your parents for their **consent**. You will be of our help, won't you?" Catherine **nodded** and Isabella continued, "We have so little money. Your parents may not like it. But we'll know everything tomorrow. Oh, I can't wait!"

Catherine spent a couple of days cheering up her friend in **suspension**. Two days later, a letter arrived from James announcing good news:

My dearest Isabella,

My parents agreed that we can be married. They kindly promised to do all they can do to help us in our happiness.

with all my love,
James Morland ◆

The letter was short, but Isabella did not need to inquire any further. It satisfied her to imagine herself in a few weeks being a lovely bride of James Morland. Isabella also imagined herself wearing a new lace gown, with rings upon her fingers, being helped by a maid and riding on a new carriage. She wanted to be **admired** by everybody in Fullerton.

John Thorpe, receiving this news, came to see Catherine and asked, "Do you agree with their idea of marrying?" "Of course," answered Catherine. Then he added, "Do you know an old song, 'Going to a wedding brings another'? I hope you will be pleased to see me at their wedding in Fullerton."

"Of course," Catherine answered. "It's always good to have company."

John Thorpe left, satisfied that Catherine encouraged him in his idea of marrying her.

On the other hand, Catherine felt that things were not so satisfying. Though she had been excited about going to the Tilney's for dinner, she did not enjoy it as much as she had expected; General Tilney was very kind and attentive to her, but Henry and Eleanor were so quiet that Catherine thought she might have done something wrong.

Catherine spoke to Isabella about her worry. Isabella **blamed** the Tilneys for being too proud. "They're stuck-up people, anyway," concluded Isabella. Catherine decided to see how it would turn at the dance that evening. As for Isabella, she said that it was out of the question for her to dance because she was now engaged to James.

02 Captain Tilney

Answer the following questions in Japanese as you read the story.

1 What did Frederick Tilney look like?

フレデリック・ティルニーはどんな外見をしていましたか。

2 What astonished Catherine?

キャサリンはなぜびっくり仰天したのですか。

3 What was the reason Isabella gave Catherine for changing her mind to dance?

イザベラは、気が変わって踊る理由をどう述べましたか。

That evening, another male member of Tilney family appeared at the dance — Captain Frederick Tilney. He was a fashionable, handsome man. He talked with his brother Henry and then Henry came over to Catherine. He asked if Miss Thorpe would dance with Captain Tilney.

"Oh, I don't think so. Isabella said that she wasn't coming to dance this evening in the first place. But it was kind of him to think of Isabella."

"You are so good-natured to see kindness in my brother's action. I'm sure he has other reasons to have thought of Miss Thorpe."

Though Catherine was a little at a loss, she pleased to hear Henry's **compliment**. But a few minutes later, she was **astonished** to see Isabella walking onto the dancing floor escorted by Captain Tilney. Isabella's eyes met Catherine's and she **shrugged** her shoulders.

Later, Catherine had a chance to ask Isabella. "What changed your mind?" Isabella shrugged her shoulders again and said, "Why, he wouldn't take no for answer. He wouldn't leave me until he heard yes." While Catherine could not say a word, Isabella added, "He is so dashing. Everybody was watching us."

03 Isabella complains

Answer the following questions in Japanese as you read the story.

1 What did another letter from James tell?

もう一通のジェイムズからの手紙には何が書かれていましたか。

2 How long should Isabella Thorpe and James Morland wait till their marriage?

イザベラ・ソープとジェイムズ・モーランドは、結婚するまでどれほどの時を待たねばなりません。

3 Why did Isabella complain about the money Mr. Morland promised to provide? State both Isabella's explanation and Catherine's hopeful interpretation.

イザベラはなぜモーランド氏が与えると約束したお金に不平を言ったのでしょう。イザベラ自身の説明と、キャサリンの希望的解釈を述べましょう。

(2-3)

While Catherine was with Isabella at Mrs. Thorpe's, Isabella received another letter from James. It contained a **subject** more interesting than a dance; Mr. Morland offered four hundred pounds a year as soon as James should be old enough to marry. Considering that Mr. Morland had ten children, this was quite a **generous** offer. But the message of the letter also meant that Isabella and James had to wait for two years before their marriage.

"I'm sure Mr. Morland has been most generous, but four hundred pounds is not enough for starting a new life. I wish he can do more later." said Mrs. Thorpe. "Well, everybody has the right to do what he likes with his money," said Isabella.

Catherine was shocked to hear how they talked about her father. Isabella said, "You know, it is not myself that I care for. I never care about myself. I'm thinking about James." To hear this, Catherine tried to believe Isabella complained about money because she was anxious to marry James without waiting for long.

» Reviewing the story

Ⅰ • Reorder a)〜e) according to the story.

a) Isabella declared that she would not dance now that she was engaged with James.

b) Catherine came to know that her brother was engaged with Isabella Thorpe.

c) Catherine was shocked to hear how Isabella and Mrs. Thorpe talked about her own father.

d) Catherine told Isabella that she had not enjoyed herself so much at the dinner with the Tilneys.

e) Catherine was surprised to see Isabella dance with Captain Frederick Tilney.

Ⅱ • Complete the sentences using the given words.

generous	blamed	suspension	compliment	shrugged

1 Catherine was so naive that she was pleased to hear Henry's [   ] on her good nature.

2 Isabella had been in a state of [   ] till she received the letter from James.

3 Isabella [   ] the Tilneys for being too proud.

4 Isabella [   ] her shoulders when her eyes met Catherine's.

5 Mr. Morland made a [   ] arrangement in providing for his son and daughter-in-law.

» Listening and oral practices

Fill the blanks as you listen and practice the conversation with your partner.

A : Will Miss Thorpe dance with Frederick?

B : I don't think so, for Isabella said that [¹   ] this evening in the first place.

A : Are you sure?

B : Yes. But [²   ] Isabella.

A : You are so good-natured to [³   ]. Everybody except you knows he has [⁴   ] Miss Thorpe.

» Tips for reading

完了助動詞　「今」の主観を表す助動詞より前のこと、すでに結果がでていること、ある

いは「今」もしくは直前まで続いてきたことを完了形で表す。

Catherine thought she **might have done** something wrong.

キャサリンは、自分は何かいけないことを<u>したのかもしれない</u>、と思った。

    must have ＋過去分詞＝したに違いない

    should/ought to have ＋過去分詞＝本来ならしたはずである、すべきだったのにしていない

    may/might have ＋過去分詞＝したのかもしれない（may は might より可能性が高い）

注）must≒have to「しなくてはいけない」であるが、一方、must not「してはいけない」と not have to=need not を区別すること。

▶ 英語を完成しましょう。

1）Not only Henry but also other people in the ball room ［　　　　　　　　　］ Frederick's intention with young women like Isabella.

ヘンリーばかりかダンス室の他の人々も、イザベラのような若い女性に対するフレデリックの思うところを知っていたかもしれない。

2）James ［　　　　　　　　　］ his date more wisely.

ジェイムズは恋人をもっと賢く選ぶべきだった。

3）Isabella ［　　　　　　　　　］ the Morland family richer than they really were.

イザベラはモーランド家がじっさいよりお金持ちだと思ったにちがいない。

◀ **「of ＋抽象名詞 ＝ 形容詞」** ▶ の場合

You will be **of our help**. ＝ You will be **helpful to us**.

Henry's father was **a man of importance**. ⇒ Henry's father was **an important man**.

▶ 形容詞を使って英語を完成しましょう。

Catherine had an impression that Henry was **a man of intelligence**.

⇒ Catherine had an impression that Henry was ［　　　　　　　　　］.

John wanted to make sure that Mr. Allen was **a man of wealth** with no children.

⇒ John wanted to make sure that Mr. Allen was ［　　　　　　　　　］ with no children.

◀ **as for～** ▶ ＝ about （as for～は人に言及。モノ・事は as to～。）

Visitors to Bath might have various ambitions. **As for** Mr. Allen, it is enough to drink water from the mineral spring and relax for a while.

▶ 英語を完成しましょう。

［　　　　　　　　　］, it was John who knew a lot while ［　　　　　　　　　］ Mrs. Allen, she has her personal views about ladies' gowns.

馬と犬に関して詳しいのはジョンで、アレン夫人といえばドレスに一家言もっている。

参考）as for はカジュアルな表現。フォーマルな文書や会話では regarding / in terms of / concerning などを使おう。

◀ out of the question ▶　「とんでもない」「問題外である」（但し out of question = no doubt「疑いない」）

▶ out of question または out of the question のどちらかを入れて英文を完成しましょう。

It was really [¹　　　　　　　　　　　] for Isabella to dance with Captain Tilney. But she danced with him and enjoyed attracting the onlookers' attention. That she is not so sincere is [²　　　　　　　　　].

❯❯ Read a part of the original passage

"It is not on my own account I wish for more; but I cannot bear to be the means of injuring my dear Morland, making him sit down upon an income hardly enough to find one in the common necessaries of life. For myself, it is nothing; I never think of myself."
(…) "Nobody can think better of Mr. Morland than I do, I am sure. But everybody has their failing, you know, and everybody has a right to do what they like with their own money." Catherine was hurt by these insinuations. "I am very sure," said she, "that my father has promised to do as much as he can afford."

❯❯ Write a passage as a character

Write a passage of 3〜6 sentences from Isabella's diary about the content of the letter from James and her dancing with Captain Frederick Tilney.

column 06 　ダンディの時代の男性服

1800年代の男性用正装の例

ヴィクトリア＆アルバート
博物館所蔵の摂政時代の男
性服

ロココからの脱却

　ジェイン・オースティンの作家活動の時期はおおよそ「摂政時代（Regency era / Regency period）」に重なります。これは狭義には、難病（おそらくポルフィリン症）によって政務を執れなくなった父王ジョージ3世に代わり皇太子（後のジョージ4世）が摂政となった1811年から1820年を、また多くの場合もっと広く、1770年代からジョージ4世が崩御した1837までを指します。

　このころ、建築や内装や食器だけでなく、女性服にも一種の新古典趣味の浸透を見ました。すなわち、それまでの主にフランス産のシルクの刺繍生地を中心としたロココ・ファッションから、シルクと並んで軽い綿モスリンを多用した、古代ローマ風（あくまで想像上）の簡素な衣装や、イタリア・ルネサンスの肖像画に描かれるラインが流行しました。この変化については、「母性」という概念が捏造されるとともにウエストラインが解放されて妊婦服に近づいた、と言う分析もあります。

　では、男性たちはどんな服装をしていたのでしょう。

　この時代の男性服の土台は18世紀に確立したスタイルで、刺繍生地にレースといった装飾的なフランス風から脱してシンプルなブリティッシュ・スタイルに向かっていました。基本的には上着（coat）、ベスト（waistcoat）、シャツ、ズボン、靴下という、現代の紳士服に引き継がれている組み合わせです。ズボンは1800年前後まで

《バーボード・バーボード
男爵》（c.1783）トマス・
ゲインズバラ作

ではブリーチと呼ばれる短いものが主流で、また上着は今の燕尾服の元となったフロックコートでした。首にはクラヴァットという、ネクタイの元となった衿布を巻いていました。ヘンリー・ティルニーを始め、『ノーサンガー・アビー』に登場する男性たちも、軍服か聖職者の服装をのぞけばこうした装いのはずです。

ジョージ・ブランメル

　さてこのころ、男性服の流行をリードし洗練した人物がいました。ジョージ・ブランメル（1778-1840）という、貴族の秘書を父に持つ平民です。イートン校、オックスフォードと進み、学生時代からクールな立ちふるまいと非の打ちどころのない着こなし、そして当意即妙な会話で知られていました。彼の運は皇太子との出会いから上昇し始めます。皇太子は伯母の家で逢った10歳年下のブランメルに魅了され、貴族の子弟たちからなる自分のクラブのメンバーとし、のちには花形である近衛第十騎兵隊に加えました。皇太子の後ろ盾によって社交界の中心に居場所を得たブランメルの影響力はどんどん大きくなり、男性服だけでなく女性服や

ワインや食器にいたるまで、彼の好みが「ブランメル氏お墨付き」「ブランメル氏御用達」としてありがたがられるようになりました。皇太子の名前を使って借りた金でギャンブルをしてさらに借金を膨らませる、といった豪遊も看過され、それがまた「ダンディ」としての彼の名を上げたのです。

テイスト・リーダーとしての彼の価値は、ひとえにその外見の完璧さにかかっており、彼自身、「外見すなわち人間の価値」という哲学を押し通しました。思想家トマス・カーライルはブランメルが体現する「ダンディ」について、「その職業、職務、生活は服を着ることにある。その魂や精神や財布や人格の全能力が、服を抜け目なく着るという、一つの目的のために奉げられている。他の人々が生きるために服を着るのに対し、彼は服を着るために生きている」と言っています。ブランメルはどう装ったのでしょう。

ブランメルの肖像画のエッチング

彼が愛用したのはフロックコートで、これはもともと動きやすさを好んだ農夫たちから広まった上着でした。しかし上流のワードローブに加わってからは、ほとんど身にぴったり合った仕立てとなりました。簡素なカットがつくり出す禁欲的な窮屈さと、ほとんど無地無彩色のウール素材の組み合わせは、「男の清潔」を信条とする英国風を代表するアイテムとなりました。前時代に流行したフランス宮廷風とは対称的なテイストを突き詰めたと言えましょう。

ブランメルが他界した直後の伝記によると、彼は「なにげない完璧さ」のために、上着とベストとズボンを、それぞれを得意とする別々の仕立て屋に作らせ、仮縫いを重ねてフィッティングを徹底しました。いきおいボタンなどは最小限にとどめ、ひと目を引くディテールは排除しました。ブランメル曰く、「紳士にとっての最大の恥は、その外見によって人目をひくこと」なのです。

ブランメルの戯画（1805）
リチャード・ダイトン作

一番こだわったのはクラヴァットで、シャツの衿を立てて細い布を外側から巻き、前で結んで襟を折り返す——出来栄えは着る人の独創と手先にかかった、小さいながら顔と衣装の統合点として装いを仕上げるアイテムでした。ブランメル以前はレースが多かったのですが、彼はキリっとアイロンのかかったリネンや、柔らかさと光沢を調整した絹を愛用し、それらに首回りで立体的な美しさを与えることに労力を費やしました。一度結び損ねたクラヴァットはそのまま使えないのです。

ブランメルが流行させたのは座れないほど細身のズボンや彫刻的な首を要求するクラヴァットでしたが、それは肥満体には致命的でした。ブランメルはあるときジョージ４世の飽満な身体に嘲笑的なコメントをしてしまい、それから彼の運は急降下していきました。1832年、借金漬けの彼は債務執行を逃れるためカレーに移り住みます。（当時は返済

ロンドン、ジャーミン通に立つブランメルの像

ジョージ４世の戯画のエッチング ©British Museum

できない債務者は牢獄に収監されました。）1837年にジョージ4世が崩御すると、かつての取り巻きのはからいでカレー領事の地位に推挙されたりもしましたが借金は重なるばかり。いよいよカレーの債務牢獄に収監されたあと、老人救貧院へ移って半ば正気を失ったまま最期を迎えました。

　次の時代のフランスの詩人ボードレールは「現代生活の画家」という文章のなかで、「資力や家柄でなく、テイストによって社会をリードして高いステイタスを得ようとする存在」について述べています。それは、「貴族の権威の失墜が部分的で」、まだ「民主制は全能ではない」過渡期に現れ、一種の新たな貴族制を打ち立てようとする動きである、と。ブランメルの悲劇は、自らのテイストによって精神的には他者の優位に立つことを求めつつ、その優位性を認めるのは劣位に置かれるべき他者、すなわち王侯貴族たちである、という矛盾にあったのでしょう。今、高級紳士服の店が並ぶロンドンのジャーミンストリートでは、細身のフロックコートに身を包んだブランメルの像が私たちを迎えてくれます。

参考資料
『ダンディズム　栄光と悲惨』生田耕作（中央文庫 1999）
『イギリスを知るための 65 章』近藤久雄他 41-42 章（明石書店 2014）

Chapter 07

NORTHANGER ABBEY

» Get ready with vocabulary!

Match the Japanese words 1～10 with the English words given below.

1 祝福する　　2 ほっとしている　　3 隠す　　4 恭しく

5 わくわくして　　6 廊下　　7 身振り　　8 ぼんやりしている

9 伝説　　10 消す

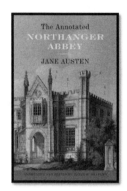

thrilled	absent-minded	legend	gesture	extinguish
bless	conceal	respectfully	relieved	corridor

» Enjoy the story!

01　An unexpected invitation

Answer the following questions in Japanese as you read the story.

1 Why was Catherine relieved?

キャサリンはなぜほっとしたのですか。

2 What did General Tilney say to Catherine at the dance?

ティルニー将軍はダンス場でキャサリンになんと言いましたか。

3 What made Catherine excited and thrilled?

キャサリンはなぜ、わくわくドキドキしたのでしょう。

2-5

　　Mr. and Mrs. Allen had been in Bath for six weeks and now they were considering going back to Fullerton. Catherine wanted to stay in Bath and continue to see Henry Tilney. Now that her brother James was engaged with Isabella, Catherine wished she also would be **blessed** with the same kind of happenings. Then the Allens decided to stay in Bath for another three weeks. Catherine felt **relieved**.

　　But soon, Catherine was to leave Bath without the Allens, and it happened like this.

　　One day, Eleanor Tilney informed Catherine that her father had decided to leave Bath at the end of the week with his family. Catherine could not **conceal** her disappointment. Then at the dance that evening, General Tilney himself invited Catherine to their country house. ◆

　　"I'd like you to stay at our home with us in Gloucestershire," he kindly said to her. "At Northanger Abbey, you can't have the same amusement as here in Bath, but we'll try to make you as comfortable as we can." Catherine **respectfully** accepted his invita-

51

tion. She was so very glad.

In fact, she was **thrilled** — Northanger Abbey! She was of course delighted to spend time in company with Henry and Eleanor. But she was excited as much about staying at an old abbey. She could not stop imagining the dark, long **corridors**, the old chapels, the hidden chambers, the secret passages, and the long-lost letters to reveal family secrets — all those things that would be found in *The Mysteries of Udolpho*.

02 Catherine worries about Isabella and Captain Tilney

Answer the following questions in Japanese as you read the story.

1 Who was Isabella Thorpe probably waiting for in the Pump Room?

イザベラ・ソープがパンプ・ルームで待っていたのはおそらく誰だったのでしょう。

2 What was written in the letter from John Thorpe, according to his sister?

妹によればジョン・ソープは手紙に何と書いていましたか。

3 Why did Catherine leave Isabella Thorpe with Captain Tilney?

キャサリンはどうしてイザベラ・ソープとティルニー大佐をおいて場を離れたのでしょう。

Catherine's mind was occupied with Northanger Abbey which she hadn't seen yet. So she was not aware that a few days had passed without seeing Isabella since she accepted the invitation from the General.

On the third day, Catherine found Isabella in the Pump Room. She was constantly watching the entrance door. She noticed Catherine and called her by **gesture**.

"Don't worry, Isabella. James is coming soon," said Catherine walking up to her.

"Oh, I'm not watching for him. I have something to tell you." Isabella then looked around the room. "I'm not waiting for anybody. Anybody in particular."

"What was it that you wanted to tell me?" asked Catherine.

"Oh, yes, Captain Tilney says I'm very **absent-minded**. I had just received a letter from John."

"Yes?"

"You know what is written in the letter."

"No, what is it?"

"About you, of course. He is in love with you!"

"With me?" Catherine thought of the excursions and the conversations she had had with John Thorpe. "No, I don't think so. And if so, I am sorry, for I don't feel the same about him."

"Oh, don't answer in a haste. You know, you feel one thing one day and the next day everything changes. Captain Tilney says people often don't understand their feelings. Oh, here he comes!"

Captain Frederick Tilney, seeing Catherine standing next to Isabella, looked somewhat annoyed. So Catherine left Isabella, who immediately sat with Frederick. To Catherine, he seems to be falling in love with Isabella and Isabella seemed to encourage him — only unconsciously. "She doesn't know what she is doing", Catherine thought, because Isabella was engaged with James. Still, Catherine wished Isabella had not looked so obviously delighted to see Captain Tilney. She also wished Isabella had not talked about his father and his money in that way.

03 Catherine listens to Henry

Answer the following questions in Japanese as you read the story.

1 What was Henry's advice to Catherine who was worried about James and Isabella?

ジェイムズとイザベラのことを心配するキャサリンに、ヘンリーはどんなアドバイスをしましたか。

2 Basically, where does Henry Tilney live?

ヘンリー・ティルニーは普段はどこに住んでいるのでしょう。

3 Why could not Henry Tilney continue to describe Northanger Abbey?

ヘンリー・ティルニーはどうしてノーサンガー・アビーについて話し続けることができなかったのでしょう。

(2-7)

Catherine confessed her worries about Isabella and Captain Tilney to Henry Tilney.
"So you think it is my brother who makes your brother unhappy," said Henry.
"Yes. I'm afraid so."

"Henry drove so well" Chap XX

"To be more exact, which is it that's bothering you? The attention my brother gives to Miss Thorpe or the way she receives it?"

"Well, I don't know."

"You know, if some other men admire a man's fiancée, the man would feel rather flattered as long as she behaves decently. So, don't worry. Leave the matter to your brother and Isabella Thorpe. They can take care of themselves. I'm sure they will soon laugh about it."

The day came to leave Bath for Northanger Abbey. Catherine and Henry rode in one carriage and Eleanor and General Tilney in the other. Captain Tilney remained in Bath, which cast a little shadow on Catherine's mind.

Henry said he was so glad for Eleanor that Catharine would stay with her because she had been a little lonely; General Tilney was often away.

"Don't you live with her?" asked Catherine.

"Not always. I have a house of my own in Woodston, more than thirty kilometres away from Northanger Abbey."

This triggered Catherine. She could not wait a moment longer to ask him to describe Northanger Abbey. Henry understood her romantic view of what old abbeys were like, so he told stories about it, both from its history and its **legends** with mysteries. He was very amused to see that his stories evidently fed her imagination.

"One of our maids might tell you that your room is haunted."

"Oh, and then?"

"On the second or the third night after your arrival, you may hear a violent storm with a flash of thunder. A gust of wind comes into your room and you may notice a part of the hangings moving unnaturally, for your lamp isn't **extinguished** yet."

"Oh no! Stop! Well, yes, go on, what happens then?"

Henry, trying to suppress his laugh, could not continue his story.

» Reviewing the story

I • Reorder a)～e) according to the story.

a) Catherine witnessed Isabella and Captain Tilney getting close each other.

b) Mr. and Mrs. Allen decided to remain in Bath for another three weeks.

c) General Tilney invited Catherine to his mansion in Gloucester.

d) Catherine was thrilled to listen to Henry's description of Northanger Abbey.

e) Catherine talked with Henry Tilney of her worries about Isabella and Captain Tilney.

II • Complete the sentences using the given words.

suppress	corridors	conceal	respectfully	legends

1 Catherine could not [   ] her disappointment to hear Henry and Eleanor were leaving Bath.

2 Catherine [   ] accepted the invitation from General Tilney.

3 Catherine imagined some long dark [   ] and secret rooms of Northanger Abbey.

4 Henry Tilney teased Catherine by narrating to her the mysteries and [   ] of Northanger Abbey.

5 Henry Tilney, seeing Catherine's reaction to his narration, had to [   ] a laugh.

» Listening and oral practices

Fill the blanks as you listen and practice the conversation with your partner.

(2-8)

A : So, you think it is my brother who makes your brother unhappy.

B : [¹   ].

A : [²   ], which is it that's bothering you? The attention my brother gives to Miss Thorpe or [³   ].

B : Well, I don't know.

A : You know, if a man's fiancée is admired by other men, he should feel rather flattered [⁴   ]. Don't worry, leave the matter to your brother and Isabella.

» Tips for reading

◀ Now that~ ▶ 「今や～であるからには」

Now that her brother James was engaged with Isabella,….

▶ [ ] 内を並び替えて文を完成しましょう。文頭は大文字に。

"[to claim a part of the property / I should be entitled / I'm to be his wife, / now that] the Morland family have in Fullerton," Isabella thought.

◀ It...that (which) / It...who (whom) の強調構文 ▶

So, **it** is my brother **who** makes your brother unhappy.

じゃ、君のお兄さんを不幸せにしているのは僕の兄なんだね。

▶ 次の文の主語、副詞、目的語それぞれを強調する英文に直しましょう。

The sound of "Northanger Abbey" instantly thrilled Catherine.

主語 [   ].

副詞 [   ].

目的語 [   ].

◄ 独立不定詞 ►

To be more exact, which is it that is bothering you?

もっと厳密に言うと、君を悩ましているのはどちらなんだい。

To Catherine's surprise, Isabella seemed to be encouraging Captain Tilney to fall in love with her. キャサリンが驚いたことにイザベラはティルニー大佐に恋させようとしているようでした。

▶ 選択肢を使って英文を完成しましょう。

to be frank / needless to say / so to speak / to make the matter worse

It is obvious to you readers, isn't it? [¹   ], Isabella is encouraging Captain Tilney. She is, [²   ], a flirt. [³   ], Captain Tilney is also seducing Isabella. He is a typical playboy. Catherine, however, does not want to admit it. Or [⁴   ] with you, she is a bit slow.

　読者の皆さんはお分かりですね。言うまでもなくイザベラはティルニー大佐を誘っています。彼女はいわゆる尻軽なのです。さらにいけないことにティルニー大佐もまたイザベラを誘っています。典型的なプレイボーイですね。しかしキャサリンはそれを認めたくないのです。あるいはざっくばらんに言うと、彼女はちょっと鈍いのですね。

◄ 理由の接続詞 ", for" ►　「というのも」「なぜなら」

▶ 日本語に訳しましょう。

"And if so, I am sorry, **for** I don't feel the same about him." 注）この場合 if＝even if

---

» Read a part of the original passage

"Nothing further to alarm perhaps may occur the first night. After surmounting your unconquerable horror of the bed, you will retire to rest, and get a few hours' unquiet slumber. But on the second, or at farthest the third night after your arrival, you will probably have a violent storm. Peals of thunder so loud as to seem to shake the edifice to its foundation will roll round the neighbouring mountains— and during the frightful gusts of wind which accompany it, you will probably think you discern (for your lamp is not extinguished) one part of the hanging more violently agitated than the rest."

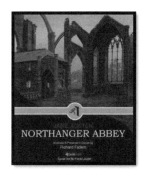

» Write a passage as a character

Write a passage of 3〜6 sentences from Henry's diary mentioning Catherine's reactions to his description of Northanger Abbey.

column 07 　僧院「アビー」の廃墟

新旧の建築スタイル

　『ノーサンガー・アビー』でキャサリンは、ブレイズ城の見物につられ、ティルニー兄妹を待ちきれずジョン・ソープたちと出かけてしまいましたね。実は18世紀、ゴシック小説の流行に先駆けて、その舞台を連想させる古い建物や場所が人々の興味を引いた時期がありました。主のいなくなった城や僧院（修道院）などの廃墟です。また同じころ死を詠う「哀歌（挽歌）」の流行もありました。これらは総じて「滅びの美」の成立を示唆しているのかもしれません。

　ジェインの時代、18世紀後半から19世紀前半はことに僧院や聖堂の廃墟が人々を引き付けたようです。イングランドでは、ヘンリー8世（在位1509-1547）がローマ教会と決別したとき各地でそうしたローマ教会関連の宗教施設が破壊されたのですが、これらの廃墟はそれ以前の「古きよきイングランド」へのノスタルジーを感じさせ、これもまた隆盛しつつあった風景画の多くに描かれました。アビー（abbey）とは僧院だけでなく、かつて僧院があった地も指す言葉です。Northanger Abbey というタイトルが僧院などを舞台とするゴシック小説のパロディ化を示す（コラム1参照）のは明らかですが、当時の廃墟ブームを思えば、「ノーサンガー・アビー」というティルニー家の屋敷名を聞いて、ゴシック小説ファンのキャサリンが勝手にあれこれ盛りあがってしまうのも無理はないのです。

　しかしながらコラム1で触れたように、18世紀後半にはイタリアの建築家アンドレア・パッラーディオ（1508-1580）に傾倒するジョン・ウッド、そしてロバート・アダム（1728-1792）のデザインに代表される、直線的なデザインに古典のモチーフを取り入れたネオ・クラシシ

イングランドにおける代表的パッラーディオ
風建築の一つ、ウォーバーン・アビー

ズム（新古典趣味）が流行します。町のシンボルの一つパルトニー橋やパンプ・ルームを始め、アダムの建築はバースにも多く残っています。グロスターシャーのティルニー邸も、「アビー」と呼ばれていながらこの流行に乗ってすっきり改装されているようで、ゴシック小説に登場する陰鬱な僧院風の内装を期待していたキャサリンは少しがっかりしていましたね。

トマス・クロムウェル ― 廃墟を作った男

　ところで、実際にイングランド各地の僧院を破壊したのはヘンリー8世ではなく、王の第一大臣だったトマス・クロムウェル（1485-1540）と、ヘンリーの息子でクロムウェルの路線を継いだプロテスタント支持の少年王、エドワード6世（1537-1553）でした。18世紀イングランドに「滅びの美」というテイストを醸成した僧院の廃墟の存在を理解するにはこのクロムウェルに触れておく必要があります。ご推察のとおり、清教徒革命の立役者オリヴァー・クロムウェル（1599-1658）の先祖です。

《トマス・クロムウェルの肖像》
（1533）ハンス・ホルバイン作

トマス・クロムウェルは、ビール屋を営む父親から虐待を受けて育ち、17歳で傭兵としてフランスへ渡ります。そしてどういう経緯かイタリア、フィレンツェの金融業者バルディ家で働くようになり、そこでフランス語イタリア語ドイツ語と、戦国領主を相手にした銀行業務を身に付け、イングランドに帰ると富裕な未亡人と結婚しました。

　さて1517年、まさにマルティン・ルターが贖宥状をめぐる疑問をマインツ司教にぶつけたこの年、イングランドの羊毛組合はローマ教会から与えられていた贖宥状独占販売許可の期限を迎えていました。いわば、濡れ手で粟を保証してくれる有名ブランドとのライセンス契約が切れるところだったのです。クロムウェルは、組合の依頼によって、メディチ家出身の教皇レオ10世から贖宥状販売権の更新許可を取り付けるべくローマへ渡ります。しかしながら教皇庁の陳情の列に並ぶのではなく、狩りの帰り道で上機嫌な教皇を待ち伏せてもてなすことによってライセンス更新をとりつけました。クロムウェルは教皇レオが甘いものと音楽に目がないことをフィレンツェ時代に掴んでおり、イングランドから連れてきたコーラス隊と、砂糖と香辛料たっぷりの菓子を用意していたのです。教皇とはイタリア語で恭しく話をしたことでしょう。

南ウェールズに残るティンターン・アビーの廃墟

　しかしながらクロムウェルは実はコアな反カソリックで、羊毛組合の免罪符ビジネスに協力したのはイングランドの金がローマ教会に吸い取られるのを阻むためでした。このあと彼は「教皇と直接交渉できる」フィクサーとして、ヘンリー8世の側近ウルジーのもとにかかえられ、1532年、いよいよ王の第一大臣となると、イングランド各地にローマ教会が持っていた僧院を次々と破壊して解散させ、その富を接収して国内の教育事業や貧困者救済、プロテスタント国への留学生派遣などに使ったのです。行き場を失った修道僧たちへの年金も忘れませんでした。

　僧院を破壊するにあたってクロムウェルは、ローマ教会に支配されていた史実を後世のイングランドの民に伝えて教訓とするため、巨大な壁など、自国におけるかつてのカトリックの権勢を伝える建物の一部を意図的に残しました。それが時を経て廃墟となったのです。クロムウェル自身は、王の4人目の妃として自分がクレーフェから連れてきたアンが王の好みでなかったことで王の不興を買い、志半ばで首を落とされてしまいます。しかし彼が残した僧院の廃墟は、ローマ教会を恐れる必要のない大国に成長した後世のイングランドで大ブームとなりました。滅びの美を伝えるその情景は、絵画のみならず多くの詩や小説にも描かれ、そして今や世界中から人々をひきつける観光資源となっているのです。

参考資料
『ロンドン・ナショナル・ギャラリー　名画がささやく激動の歴史』7章　細川祐子（2020 明石書店）

» Get ready with vocabulary!

Match the Japanese words 1～10 with the English words given below.

1 悪いことが起こりそうな　　2 つつがなく・無事に　　3 雰囲気

4 抑えられた　　5 寝返りを打つ　　6 まさぐる　　7 請求書

8 壮麗な　　9 悪漢　　10 疲れきっている

| grope | exhausted | foreboding | splendid | villain |

| uneventfully | restrained | atmosphere | bill |

| toss and turn |

» Enjoy the story!

01 The first night at Northanger Abbey

Answer the following questions in Japanese as you read the story.

1 What was the first impression Catherine had on arriving at Northanger Abbey?
ノーサンガー・アビーに到着してキャサリンはまずどんな印象を受けたでしょう。

2 What was the weather like on the first night at Northanger Abbey? How did Catherine feel?
滞在の最初の晩の天候はどうでしたか。キャサリンはどう感じましたか。

3 What did Catherine find in the old chest?
古いチェストのなかにキャサリンは何を見つけましたか。

2-9

When Catherine finally arrived at Northanger Abbey, she found the place not so dark nor **foreboding** as she had expected. Rather, it was light and orderly with large windows.

She was shown to her room and left there to change for dinner. The room looked comfortable and clean. As soon as she was alone, however, she began to examine each corner of it looking for a secret door. She could not find any.

Soon Eleanor came to take her to the dinner table, where General Tilney and Henry were waiting. Though the dinner

proceeded **uneventfully**, Henry and Eleanor were very quiet when the General was with them. The **atmosphere** at the table was a little **restrained** despite the kindness and consideration the Tilneys showed to her. ◆

When she went back to her room, the fire was burning and it was warm. Though a storm was beginning to roar outside, Catherine felt secure. As she prepared her bed, she found an old chest beside it. The key was in its hole, so she decided to look inside.

Catherine spent some time trying to open the chest but it was not easy. A gust of wind came in through the fireplace chimney and extinguished her lamp. She finally gave up and went to bed. Naturally, she could not sleep. The storm was raging outside. She **tossed and turned** for a couple of hours and finally fell asleep before dawn.

When Catherine woke up the next morning, a maid was opening the curtains and the fire was already lit. As soon as the maid went out, she began to work on opening the chest again. The keyhole made a small sound and the lid moved a little. She could not fully open it, however. She could only **grope** the inside through the slit. Her fingers touched a roll of paper. With some more efforts she opened the lid and took it out. The paper looked very old and something was written on it.

02 Catherine admires the place

Answer the following questions in Japanese as you read the story.

1 What were the pieces of old paper that Catherine found in the chest?

チェストの中にキャサリンが見つけた古い紙は何だったでしょう。

2 What was Catherine told at breakfast?

キャサリンは朝食の席で何を告げられましたか。

3 What pleased General Tilney?

ティルニー将軍は何を喜びましたか。

She brought it into the light from the window and realized that it was not a roll of paper. It was shorter pieces rolled up inside one another and wrapped up in an old sheet of paper. The first piece was — a **bill**. A bill for laundry; bed sheets, pillowcases, clothes…. The second piece was a bill for candles. They were all bills for various domestic services, such as laundries and hairdressers and so on.

How silly she was! She put the bills back in the drawer and just hoped Henry Tilney would never know what she had done on the first night at Northanger Abbey.

At breakfast, she was told that Henry had returned to his house in Woodston. She was keen to see all the rooms, towers, and passages. In fact, the General had promised

the previous night to show them to her. But since it was such a lovely morning with the sky clear after the storm, he decided to show her around the gardens on the property first. Eleanor came with them.

The building was surrounded with old trees. Its sight from the lawn was so **splendid** that Catherine gasped and sighed. Her admiration of the place made the General very pleased. Next, he showed her his kitchen garden. She had never seen a kitchen garden so large, nor so many people working in one. Again, the General was pleased to

hear how impressed she was. He left Catherine to his daughter.

03 About Mrs. Tilney

Answer the following questions in Japanese as you read the story.

1 Where did Eleanor take Catherine to walk?

エレノアは散歩をしにキャサリンをどこへ連れて行ったでしょう。

2 What came to Catherine's mind while thinking about Mrs. Tilney?

ティルニー夫人のことを想っていてキャサリンは何を思い出したでしょう。

3 Why did General Tilney insist that Catherine should return to the house and rest?

キャサリンはすぐ邸へ帰って休むよう、ティルニー将軍が強く言ったのはなぜでしょう。(2-11)

Catherine then realized how she was relieved when the General was gone.

Eleanor suggested taking her favourite walk. "I love this path." She said walking through the trees. "I used to take a walk here with my mother. She passed away when I was away from home. I was thirteen."

"You must miss her a lot," she said to Eleanor.

Catherine had never heard Mrs. Tilney mentioned before. She wondered why Eleanor nor Henry had never talked about their mother, at least in the presence of the General; Eleanor had been so quiet at dinner on the previous night. "Eleanor might have been afraid of revealing to the General that she still cherishes the memories of her mother. The General didn't walk this way. He might have avoided this path." Catherine could not help recalling how in *The Mysteries of Udolpho* the aunt of the heroine was cruelly treated by her husband; the **villain** married the aunt for money in the novel.

"Mrs. Tilney brought a huge dowry to the General," Catherine remembered. "The General probably married her for it. He must have been a cruel husband." Just as Catherine jumped to this conclusion in her mind, the General himself appeared and joined his guest. Catherine also remembered, "The castles that appeared in the novel were also among the old trees."

Catherine could no longer enjoy the walk nor admire the place. She looked **exhausted**. In fact, she was exhausted. The General noticed this change in Catherine. So, he insisted that they should return to the house and rest. Then he called back Eleanor and told not to take Catherine around the inside of the Abbey until he was with them later.

» Reviewing the story

I • Reorder a)~e) according to the story.

a) Eleanor told Catherine that she had been away from home when her mother had died.

b) Catherine found Northanger Abbey unexpectedly clean and comfortable.

c) The General and Eleanor guided Catherine around the gardens on the property.

d) The papers in the chest turned out to be old bills for housework services.

e) Catherine could not fall asleep for some time with the mysterious chest by her bed.

II • Complete the sentences using the given words.

exhausted	tossed and turned	villain	foreboding	restrained

1 Catherine had expected Northanger Abbey to be somewhat dark and [   ].

2 The atmosphere at the supper table with General Tilney was [   ].

3 Catherine could not get to sleep and [   ] on the bed for a while.

4 Listening to Eleanor's story about her mother, Catherine thought of the [   ] character in *The Mysteries of Udolpho*.

5 Since Catherine looked [   ], the General delayed the tour around his mansion till later.

» Listening and monologue practices

Fill the blanks as you listen and practice the monologue.

"Mrs. Tilney brought a huge dowry to the General. He [¹   ]. Today he did not want to walk the path with Eleanor. [²   ], Eleanor was not with her. Oh, [³   ] by Mrs. Radcliffe were also among the old trees. The General [⁴   ] like the villain in the novel."

» Tips for reading

◀「名詞＋ly」の形容詞▶

Rather, it was light and **orderly**. むしろそれは明るく整然としていた。

▶ 選択肢 brotherly / lovely / lively / beastly / manly/ orderly を使って英文を完成しましょう。

At Northanger Abbey, Catherine's room was [¹   ] and comfortable. Henry was [²   ] and attractive. Catherine noticed his gentle, [³   ] care given to Eleanor. In the wood on the property, she heard [⁴   ] songs of birds. The blooming flowers along the paths were fresh and [⁵   ]. But Catherine sensed something [⁶   ] about the Abbey, or rather about its owner General Tilney.

◀ S / V / O / C の文のなかで O/C が受動を内包する場合 ▶

Catherine / had never heard / <u>Mrs. Tilney</u> / mentioned. ("Mrs. Tilney was mentioned." を内包)

キャサリンは<u>ティルニー夫人について言及される</u>のを聞いたことがなかった。

Her admiration of his place / made / <u>the General</u> / satisfied with the tour. ("The General was satisfied with the tour." を内包)

彼女が<u>土地屋敷を賛美した</u>ので<u>将軍は案内したことに満足した</u>。

　参考）無生物主語はしばしば副詞的に訳すとよい。

　<u>A few hours of ride</u> didn't bring them to Blaise Castle.

　<u>数時間乗っても</u>ブレイス城に着かなかった。

▶ 英語を完成しましょう。

1) Catherine found [   ] in the chest just before she had noticed [   ] by the gust.
   キャサリンは、風で火が消されそう（almost）なのに気づく直前、古い紙が巻かれているのを見つけた。

2) The General could not leave [   ] outside.
   将軍はキャサリンを疲れ切ったまま外にいさせておくわけにいかなかった。

A moment's glance was enough to satisfy Catherine that her apart-
ment was very unlike the one which Henry had endeavoured to
alarm her by the description of it. It was by no means unreasonably

large and contained neither
tapestry nor velvet. The walls

were papered, the floor was carpeted; the windows were
neither less perfect nor more dim* than those of the
drawing-room below; the furniture, though not of the latest
fashion, was handsome and comfortable, and the air of
the room altogether far from uncheerful.

*more dim = dimmer

Write a passage of 3〜5 sentences from Catherine's diary about her impression of General
Tilney.

column 08 作者ジェイン・オースティンのこと (1)

スティーブントンの牧師館

　ジェインは 1775 年、イングランドのハンプシャー
州スティーブントン村に、ジョージ・オースティン
と妻カッサンドラの第 7 子として生まれました。兄
弟 6 人に姉 1 人、そしてジェインと父母という家族
構成です。父は、この村と隣のディーン地区を合わ
せた教区を担当する英国国教会牧師で、ジェインは
41 年の人生のうち 25 年間を生家の牧師館で過ごし
ました。この牧師館には父の「寺子屋」の教え子数
人が住まい、また近所の人たちや親戚や兄弟の友人

スティーブントン牧師館

が出入りしていました。人間観察にはもってこいの場ですね。ただ牧師館の場所の記録はある
ものの建物は残っていません。
　家系的には母方リー家も父方オースティン家も裕福でした。とはいえジェイン自身の生家
の安定収入は父の薄給だけで、当時はめずらしくないことですが野菜を育て鶏や牛を飼い、大
家族を養うため食料の自給に努めていました。ジェインが「乳しぼりの女の子が来てくれる」
とその作業から解放されることを喜んで書き残していることから、彼女自身も家畜の世話や農
作業を手伝っていたことがうかがえます。

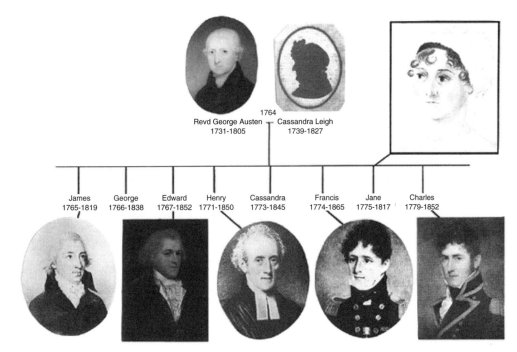

1764
Revd George Austen
1731-1805 ‑ Cassandra Leigh
1739-1827

James
1765-1819

George
1766-1838

Edward
1767-1852

Henry
1771-1850

Cassandra
1773-1845

Francis
1774-1865

Jane
1775-1817

Charles
1779-1852

オースティン家 ©Genealogy Corner

　25才以降ジェインは南イングランドで住まいを数回変え、また親戚の家など数か所に滞在しました。どこでどんな風に暮らしたのか、誰のもとを訪ねたのかをたどると彼女の創作の背景が見えてきます。「平穏な狭い世界に生きてそれを描いた」とされる作家ですが、経済的な側面を見ても、人も羨む富と安定にもう一歩のところから、事実上の貧困状態までとその振れ幅は決して小さくはなく、また恋や「結婚の打算」もあり、心のうちは大いに冒険に満ちていたと思われます。

ジェインの携帯用書き物机
©British Library

　そうしたエピソードの多くを作品に織り込んだわけですが、実は比較的平穏だった少女時代にすでに創作を始めていました。父は牧師ながら、その書棚には放蕩者の冒険を描く『トム・ジョーンズ』（*The History of Tom Jones, a Foundling*, 1749）をはじめ小説がずらりと並び、子どもたちはそれらを自由に読むことを許されていました。ジェインは読むだけでなく、十代前半から小説や脚本、歴代の王や女王の「私家版」伝記を書いて家族や友人を楽しませました。娘の才能を認めた父は執筆台を買い与え、ジェインはそれを長く愛用しました。折りたためば読書台になり、文具を入れて持ち運べる便利なものです。

　家族のうちでとりわけ親しかったのは、母の名を継ぐ2つ違いの姉カッサンドラで、姉に宛てた手紙はジェインを知る大きな手がかりとなっています。家族によるとジェインは、「カッサンドラの首が刎ねられたら自分の首も刎ねてくれと言いだしかねない」くらい姉を慕っていました。ともに1783年、オックスフォードのカウリー夫人の寄宿学校に入り、1785年に夫人が学校をサザンプトンへ移転すると姉妹いっしょに移ります。二人はこの港町で流行ったチフスに罹患し、あやうく命を落としそうになって故郷に連れ戻されますが、そのあとも揃ってレディングの寄宿学校に入っています。姉はのちに父の教え子の一人と婚約しますが、この男性

は結婚資金を作りにカリブに赴いて黄熱病で亡くなってしまいました。

　結局独身だった姉妹は、互いが人生の伴侶でした。姉は一番の理解者で、ジェインの晩年も傍にいて最期を看取りました。姉はまたジェインを描いたスケッチを残しています。似ている、似ていないと諸説ありますが、ジェインの作品や手紙を読むと、これは彼女の内面をうかがわせる肖像に思えます。

姉カッサンドラ作と見られるジェイン・オースティンの肖像

20才の恋と作家への道

　ジェインの若き日の恋について触れておきましょう。スティーブントンの牧師館に暮らしていた1796年、20歳のときの11月8日、彼女は地元の名家ディーン・ハウスで催されるちょっとした舞踏会に出席しました。それは特別な催しでもジェインの初めての舞踏会でもなく、年に数度催される地元のダンスパーティの一つにすぎませんでした。（ダンスの流行についてはコラム4参照）しかしジェインはここで、アイルランド生まれのトマス（トム）・ルフロイ（Thomas Lefroy）という青年と出会い、おそらく恋に落ちました。

　ジェインは姉にあてた手紙で、別のダンスパーティにおける自分たちのようすをこう報告しています。"I am almost afraid to tell you how my Irish friend and I behaved. Imagine to yourself everything most profligate and shocking in the way of dancing and sitting down together." ふたりは人目をはばからず親しくふるまっていたようですね。そしてトムについて、"He is a very gentlemanlike, good-looking, pleasant young man, I assure you." と描写しています。まさに『ノーサンガー・アビー』でキャサリンがヘンリー・ティルニーに抱いた第一印象のようです。いっしょにダンスに行ったりトムがオースティン家を訪問したり、交際は一年ほど続きました。

　トム・ルフロイはどんな青年だったのでしょう。ジェインと出会ったとき、彼はダブリン大学のトリニティ・カレッジで法律の勉強を終えたところでした。後援者である叔父のもとへ帰って司法試験に備える前に、スティーブントン村近くのアッシという村の牧師館に招かれて少し休息をとっていたのです。彼は先述の小説『トム・ジョーンズ』のファンで、自分と同名の主人公の派手な衣装と同じ色の上着を着てジェインに会いにくるような茶目っ気がありました。二人の会話は弾んだことでしょう。

　しかしトム・ルフロイの両親はジェインとの交際に反対でした。このころのイングランドはまだ、生まれた瞬間に将来の身分と経済的安定度がほぼ予測できる社会で、結婚はそれを変えてくれる数少ない機会の一つでした。息子が多いルフロイ家は、長男トムを裕福な家の娘と結婚させる必要があったのです。

　結局トムは、最後に会ったときにもジェインに求婚することなく、両親によってスティーブントンから遠ざけられました。二人がわれわれの推測どおりに恋をしていたなら、20才のジェインには「結婚とは恋心より、むしろ金と身分に関わる事柄である」という当時の社会の現実が身に染みたにちがいありません。この経験はしかし小説に昇華されたようです。まえがきでも触れましたが彼女の作品はすべて身分と金と結婚をめぐる心の葛藤を含み、代表作『高慢と偏見（Pride and Prejudice）』の主役ダーシーとエリザベスの造形にはトムとジェイン自身の人間性が男女を入れ替えて反映されているという分析もあります。

　ところで、ジェインはたった一日だけ婚約していたことがあります。27才の誕生日を迎え

る2週間前、1802年12月2日、家族ぐるみの付き合いがあったバッキンガムシャーのビッグ家の邸宅メニーダウンに滞在していたときのこと。ジェインは5才半年下だったハリス・ビッグ=ウィザーに求婚され、それを受け入れ、そして翌日、婚約を破棄したのです。ハリスはメニーダウン邸と領地の相続人で、ジェインを妻にと心から望んでいました。しかしジェインの姪ファニー・ナイトはハリスのことを、「冴えない外見で、おどおどと不器用なふるまいの人」と記しており、また常に紳士的というわけでもなかったようです。「叔母（ジェイン）は、彼の財産と、彼の（叔母への）愛と彼の親族への感謝から求婚を受け入れたのだろう」とファニーは推測しています。そして

ハリス・ビッグ=ウィザー

ジェイン自身、のちに、"Anything is to be preferred and endured rather than marrying without affection" と愛のない結婚を否定しています。当時まだこうした考えは主流ではなかったことを思うと、ハリスとの婚約破棄を決定したときにこれがジェインの明確な思い、彼女の「信条」となったと推測できるのではないでしょうか。

　そして、作家となって自立の道を歩むという希望を固めた時期もこのころのようです。ジェインはまもなく『レディー・スーザン（*Lady Susan*）』というデビュー作を書きあげて、1803年に10ポンドで出版社に売却しました。ところが出版社はその本を世に出すことはなく、のち1816年、ジェインの死の前年に兄ヘンリーが原稿を同額で買い戻しました。

　主人公スーザンは自分の欲するところのために偽善や策略をいとわない35才の女性で、20才台のジェインが想像で書ける人物とは思えないと考える人も多く、兄ヘンリーの結婚相手で長兄ジェイムズにも求婚されたことのあるエライザという女性がスーザンに投影されているという推測があります。エライザはオースティン家の親戚で、大革命のなかフランス人伯爵である夫がギロチンにかかったあと子どもを連れて帰国した未亡人でした。ただ、ジェインはエライザと親しくその最期を看取っています。スーザンの計算高い野心については頼もしく感じる読者もあり好悪の分かれるところですが、その策略家ぶりは軽薄に設え直してイザベラ・ソープに活かされている気がします。

　先のトム・ルフロイに話を戻すと、ユグノー（フランスの新教徒）の家系だった彼はダブリン大学に戻り、政治家、そして裁判長（大陪審院長）にまでなりました。のちにジェインの死を知ると彼女の親族を訪問し、またかつて『高慢と偏見』の出版を断った編集者からの手紙を買いとっておりまた長女をジェインと名づけていました。ジェインへの想いと敬意が一過性ではなかったことがうかがえます。

トム・ルフロイ

（次章コラムに続く）

Chapter 09

NORTHANGER ABBEY

» Get ready with vocabulary!

Match the Japanese words 1〜10 with the English words given below.

1 彫刻　　2（カーテン等の）織生地　　3 悪化する　　4 疑い

5 絶望して　　6 自分を抑える　　7 探索する　　8 立ち尽くす

9 迷う・戸惑う　　10（世話など）義務を怠っている

deteriorate	despaired	negligent	contain oneself
explore	be transfixed	sculpture	drapery	hesitate
suspicion			

» Enjoy the story!

01 The Mystery of Northanger Abbey

Answer the following questions in Japanese as you read the story.

1 Going through room after room, what did the General show and explain about to Catherine?

部屋を次々と案内して、将軍はキャサリンにどんな説明をしましたか。

2 Why was Catherine a little disappointed at first with the tour around the Abbey?

キャサリンは邸を見学して、最初なぜ少しがっかりしたのですか。

3 What was Eleanor going to show Catherine if the General had not stopped her?

もし将軍がとめなければ、エレノアはキャサリンに何を見せようとしていたのでしょう。

About an hour later, while Catherine was resting, a maid came up to her room. She notified that the General was going to conduct a tour with Eleanor around the Abbey for Catherine.

The General took Catherine through room after room and gave her the details on the furniture and the carpets, the paintings and the **sculptures**, and the fabrics and the **draperies**.

It is true that Catherine was no less impressed with the interior than with the exterior and the gardens. However, she was a little disappointed, because there were no secret rooms and passages to see. Catherine had a romantic vision of what a country house converted from an abbey should look like. The rather modern, orderly taste of the interior did not meet this vision of hers. ◆

Eleanor had gone ahead of Catharine and the General, opening the doors and windows for them. Just when Eleanor had opened a door, the General called her back angrily. "Where're you taking us?" Behind that door were more doors. Catherine wondered what were behind the doors. The part of the building suddenly seemed very interesting to her. Eleanor quickly and quietly closed the door.

Eleanor later said to Catherine, "I was going to show Mother's rooms, where she had lived and died."

"Are they kept as they used to be?"

"Yes, exactly as they used to be. It's been nine years."

"You weren't with her when she passed away, were you?"

"No, I wasn't with her. Her illness was sudden. Her condition **deteriorated** in a very short time." Eleanor sighed deeply. "I'll show you her rooms some other time." Catherine shivered.

Back in her room, she thought, "Everything had been finished when her children came back to her. Was it possible? Was it possible, like the Italian villain in the novel, the General …?" She then shivered again at the terrible **suspicion**.

02 Catherine explores the Abbey

Answer the following questions in Japanese as you read the story.

1 What was the terrible idea that Catherine held about Mrs. Tilney?

ティルニー夫人について、キャサリンはどのような恐ろしい考えを抱いたのでしょう。

2 What transfixed Catherine?

キャサリンはなぜ立ち尽くしたのですか。

3 Who unexpectedly came up the staircase?

誰が思いがけず階段を上がって来ましたか。

As Catherine lay in bed, the terrible thought came back to her. Her imagination went further; "No, perhaps she didn't die. She must be locked up behind one of the doors. That's why the General made Eleanor shut the door. Oh, what should I do? I must do something while the others are sleeping. Mrs. Tilney may be alive but weak and **despaired**. She probably receives food and water from her cruel husband."

Catherine was unable to **contain herself** and went out of her

bed to look out of the window across the courtyard. The outside was pitch-dark. She could not fall asleep, so she turned the pages of her favourite novel by a candlelight.

The next day, Catherine decided to **explore** the rooms on her own. "I have to save Mrs. Tilney. I have to see these rooms before Henry comes back." Henry was scheduled to return the following day.

She opened a door behind the first door. She **was transfixed**.

In front of her was a bright large room with a comfortable canopied bed. The sun

was streaming in through two large windows. The mahogany chest and chairs were shining. Even a few pieces of firewood were placed in the fireplace.

Catherine suddenly felt ashamed. She wanted to go back to her room to stay there alone for the rest of the day. Just as she turned around and was about to leave the part of the building, she heard some footsteps coming upstairs. She could not move. She waited, looking at the staircase.

It was Henry Tilney.

03 Henry sees through Catherine

Answer the following questions in Japanese as you nead the story.

1 Why did Henry Tilney come up the stairs?

ヘンリー・ティルニーはなぜ階段を上がってきたのでしょう。

2 What helped Henry Tilney guess that Catherine had the terrible idea about his father?

どうしてヘンリー・ティルニーは、父親についてキャサリンが恐ろしい考えを抱いていると察したのでしょう。

3 How did Catherine look up at Henry Tilney when he made the right guess at her thoughts?

キャサリンは、自分の考えをヘンリー・ティルニーが言い当てたとき、どんなふうに彼を見上げましたか。

(2-15)

"Mr. Tilney! What are you doing here? Why are you coming up these stairs?"

"Why am I coming here?" He was surprised, too. "It's because this is the quickest way from the stable to my room. And you. Why are you here?"

Catherine blushed and said, "I came here to see your mother's rooms." She looked down at the floor.

"Is there anything particular to see there?" Henry asked.

"I thought you're coming back tomorrow." Catherine said without answering his question.

"Oh, I came back as soon as possible. Did Eleanor send you here?"

"No." Catherine could not say more.

"Miss Morland, you were curious. I guess Eleanor talked about our mother a lot."

"Yes." She **hesitated** but continued. "Well, no. Miss Tilney didn't say much. But the way Mrs. Tilney died…."

"Yes?"

"Mrs. Tilney died so suddenly…and none of you were with her. Your father, ah, might not have cared about her. Ah…did he love her?"

"From these circumstances and your hesitation, I guess you imagine he had been **negligent,** or perhaps worse."

She looked up at him with fear mixed with curiosity and embarrassment.

⟫ Reviewing the story

I • Reorder a)～e) according to the story.

a) Catherine went to explore late Mrs Tilney's rooms on her own.

b) Henry Tilney rightly guessed why Catherine's curiosity was aroused.

c) Though Catherine was impressed with the art collection and the interior of the Abbey, she was a little disappointed not to see any secret passage or room.

d) Catherine unexpectedly came across Henry Tilney near his mother's bedroom.

e) General Tilney stopped Eleanor when she was about to show Catherine her mother's rooms.

II • Complete the sentences using the given words.

contain	negligent	suspicion	transfixed	sculptures

1 The General gave the detailed explanations of the [   ] and draperies.

2 Catherine had a dreadful [   ] on what had happened to Mrs. Tilney.

3 Catherine, unable to [   ] herself, went out for an exploration.

4 Catherine was [   ] to find a clean, spacious, and bright room behind the prohibited door.

5 Catherine suspected that General Tilney had been at least [   ] in the care of his wife in her illness.

» Listening and oral practices

Fill the blanks as you listen and practice the conversation with your partner.

A：Mr. Tilney! Why are you coming up these steps?

B：Why am I ···? [¹   ] to my room. And you. Why are you here?

A：Ah···to see your mother's rooms.

B：[²   ] in her rooms? Oh, you are curious, Miss Morland. Eleanor talked about our mother a lot, didn't she?

A：Well, no. Miss Tilney didn't say much.

B：Then what brought you here?

A：Well···, the way Mrs. Tilney died···. She died so suddenly and none of you were with her. Ah···, [³   ]?

B：From these circumstances and the way you hesitate, I guess you imagine [⁴   ].

» Tips for reading

◀ than を使った比較表現 ▶

Catherine was **no less** impressed with the interior **than** with the exterior.
キャサリンは屋敷まわりに劣らず（屋敷まわりと同じく）内装にも感心しました。
Catherine knew **no more** about Mrs. Tilney **than** the General knew about Catherine.
将軍がキャサリンのことを知らないのと同じく、彼女もティルニー夫人のことを知りませんでした。

▶ 並び替えて英文を作りましょう。

Catherine was disappointed because [**had an interior / than other neo-classic mansions / Northanger Abbey / no less orderly**].

▶ 以下の選択肢を使って英文を完成しましょう。

    other than ～「～の他に」
    rather（more）A than B =not so much B as A「B というよりむしろ A」
    not more than = at most ／ no more than = only
    not less than =at least ／ no less than= as much（many）as

Catherine was [¹   ] curious than inquisitive. She had never been in a big old mansion [²   ] Northanger Abbey. There were [³   ] four bedrooms in her parents' house while there seemed to be [⁴   ] a dozen of them or probably more in the Abbey.

 倒置　臨場感や強調のため、比較表現あるいは主語の説明が長い場合などにしばしばおこる。

In front of her was a bright large room with a comfortable canopied bed.
目の前には、心地よさそうな天蓋付きベッドのある明るい大きな部屋がありました。

▶ **英語を完成しましょう。**

[　　　　　　　　　　　], not with James, [　　　　　　　　　] that evening.
ジェイムズでなくティルニー大佐と、その夜イザベラは踊ったのです。

▶ [　] **内を並び替えて英文を完成しましょう。**

The more Catherine thought about Mrs Tilney, [**of Mrs. Radcliffe's novels /who was an avid reader / became Catherine / the more suspicious about the General**].
ティルニー夫人のことを考えれば考えるほど、ラドクリフ夫人の小説の熱心な読者だったキャサリンは、ますます将軍に疑いを抱きました。

≫ Read a part of the original passage

"You were with her, I suppose, to the last?"

"No," said Miss Tilney, sighing; "I was unfortunately from home. Her illness was sudden and short; and, before I arrived it was all over."

Catherine's blood ran cold with the horrid suggestions which naturally sprang from these words. Could it be possible? Could Henry's father—? And yet how many were the examples to justify even the blackest suspicions! And, when she saw him in the evening, while she worked with her friend, slowly pacing the drawing-room for an hour together in silent thoughtfulness, with downcast eyes and contracted brow, she felt secure from all possibility of wronging him. It was the air and attitude of a Montoni *!

*) Montoni = the villain in *The Mysteries of Udolpho*.

≫ Write a passage as a character

Write a passage of 3〜5 sentences from Eleanor's diary about what she did with Catherine at Northanger Abbey.

column 09 　作者ジェイン・オースティンのこと（2）

ゴッドマーシャム邸で

　前章のコラムでも触れましたが、ジェインの時代はまだ生まれた時から将来の身分と保有財産が予測できる時代でした。さて「生まれと身分と財産」と言えば、ジェインの兄エドワードは、図らずも大きな階級的飛躍を果たした稀有な例です。父のいとこで嫡子（ちゃくし）のいない富裕なナイト家の当主に気に入られ、12才で養子となったのです。実は父ジョージが牧師の地位についたのもナイト家のおかげでした。子どもたち8人のうちひとり両親に手放されたとも言えますが、ナイト家は3つの領地と邸宅をもつ旧家で、エドワードはそうした財産の多くの部分と、年15000ポンドの個人収入を保証される跡継ぎとなったのです。ちなみに『高慢と偏見』のダーシーでも年収10000ポンドという設定です。

グランドツアー先（おそらくローマ）のエドワードの肖像

　のちにジェインはケント州にあるエドワードの住まいゴッド

エドワードが相続したゴッドマーシャム邸

マーシャム邸で夏を過ごすようになり、また1808年に彼が妻を亡くしてからはさらにナイト家の子どもたちと過ごす時間が増えました。ことに姪のファニー・ナイトは叔母ジェインを慕って、ジェインについて親しく書きとめていることはすでに見ましたね。「さあ、アイスを食べてフランスワインを飲むわよ。」ゴッドマーシャム邸訪問中のジェインのこんな言葉が残っています。この邸宅は森に囲まれた涼しい窪地にあり、冬にできる氷を保存して夏のデザートに使ったりしていました。また邸の内装はまさに『ノーサンガー・アビー』でキャサリンを失望させた、あのすっきりした新古典様式です。

　ゴッドマーシャム邸に滞在中は召使に渡すチップにも不自由し、ナイト家の人々よりむしろ同家の女家庭教師とウマが合ったジェインでした。しかし、友人や親族を招いての劇の上演など、上流の社交生活を観察し参加するというこの邸（やしき）での経験がなかったなら、彼女の作品はその魅力の一部を欠くことになったでしょう。

いざ、バースへ

　1800年、父オースティン牧師は長男ジェイムズに牧師職を譲って引退します。そして妻と娘2人を連れてバースに移り住むことを決めます。娘たちの「婿探し」も念頭にあったと思われます。しかしジェインにとっては晴天の霹靂、ショックで気絶しかけたという話まで残っています。もっともこれは、人前で卒倒する女性たちを皮肉に描くジェインを茶化した言い伝えでしょう。

　ジェインはそれまでに2度バースを訪れていました。"Catherine was all eager delight; her eyes were here, there, and everywhere" とバースに目を輝かせる『ノーサンガー・アビー』の主人公とは反対に、ジェイン自身はバースを「気取って浮ついた町」と見ていました。おそらく、バースを離れて最後に執筆した『説得（*Persuasion*）』（1818）の主人公アン・エリオットが語る気持ちのほうが、ジェイン自身の思いに近いでしょう。アンは、かつて周りの意見に流されて愛する男性と別れてしまい、住んでいた邸を出て行かねばならなくなった、ジェインと重なるところがある人物です。

> 'There had been three alternatives, London, Bath, or another house in the country. All Anne's wishes had been for the latter... She disliked Bath, and did not think it agreed with her – and Bath was to be her home.'

とはいえ生活力のないジェインが親の決定に逆らうわけにはいかず、現実には、「ロンドンかバースか、どこか田舎の家か」という選択肢はありませんでした。ところで皮肉なことに、バースをアーバン・リゾートに育てた一人、初代シャンドス侯爵（1674-1744）は実はジェインの祖先にあたります。1727 年に鉱泉治療のために訪れたバースの環境が気に入り、建築家ジョン・ウッド（1704-1754）ら（1 章コラム参照）に開発を命じてサーカスやクィーン・スクエア北の住宅など「気取った」新古典主義の建築群を残しました。

いったんバース行きが決まるとジェインはしかし、母親とともに猛然と住まい探しに乗り出します。社交と体裁の町、出会いと結婚相手探しの町バースで、どのあたりに居を構えるか、それは世間の自分たちへの評価を左右し、滞在の質を決める一大事だったのです。だから『ノーサンガー・アビー』のアレン氏は、"[General Tilney's] lodgings were taken the very day after he left them, Catherine. But no wonder; Milsom-street you know" と、ティルニー家の滞在住所に言及していま

バースのミルソム通り

す。ミルソム通は今も人気エリアです。また『説得』の登場人物ヘンリエッタとルイーズ・マスグロウブは、主人公アンに、"[I]f we do go [to Bath], we must be in a good situation—none of your Queen-squares for us!" と言ったあと、"[W]hat part of Bath do you think [Sir Walter and Elizabeth] will settle in?'" と尋ねています。

では 1801 年のジェインはバースでどう動いたのでしょう。この町ではまず、母方の親戚リー・ペロット家の住むザ・パラゴン 1 番地の 4 階建テラスハウスを拠点としつつ、限られた予算で納得いく住み心地を求めてあちこちの賃貸物件を検討しました。ウエストゲイトはどこか気に入らない。チャールズ・セント・シーモアとニュー・キングス通の角は陰気くさい。小説中キャサリンがジョン・ソープの馬車からティルニー兄妹を見かけたローラ・プレイスの家は素敵だけれど家賃が高すぎる。

バースのパラゴン

グレイト・パルトニー通は心地良くない。プリンス通とチャペル横丁の角の家は、外観はいいけど内装がだめ。グリーン・パークは眺めとサイズはいいけど少し湿気がある。スクエアの 2 件も界隈はいいんだけど家が嫌。ぜったい避けたいのはトリム通の部屋で、家賃は格安だが用水路の上にあるので湿気で身体を悪くしそう。こうして最終的に落ち着いたのはシドニー・プレイス 4 番地で、オースティン一家は 3 年間の賃貸契約を結びました。当地を見学すると、す

ぐ前にシドニー・ガーデンズという公園がある明るい立地で、それも決め手だったと推察できます。

バースのシドニー・プレイス
4番地正面

　ここでの3年間、ジェインと姉カッサンドラは、故郷ハンプシャー州の友人を訪問したり、夏をケント州のゴッドマーシャム邸で過ごしたりする一方、バースの友人と行き来もし、また買い物や観劇、舞踏会と、好きでなかったはずの社交に勤しんでいました。バースでジェインの筆が進まなかったのも無理はありません。また、1803年と1804年に家族といっしょに訪れてすっかり気に入った海辺の町ライム・リージスは、のちに『説得』の舞台に取り入れられています。（この町でジェインは泡沫の恋をしたが相手の男性は早世した、とする伝記もあります。）

バースのシドニー・プレイス4
番地裏庭

　1805年、バースのシドニー・プレイスの住まいの賃貸契約期間が終了すると、オースティン一家は節約のため、以前は拒否したグリーン・パークの家に移ります。そしてしばらくするとさらに逼迫して、絶対住みたくなかったトリム通に移らざるをえなくなります。そしてこの前後、父ジョージが2日間寝込んだだけで急死してしまいます。74才で直接の死因は不明です。トリム通で容態が悪くなったとする研究者には、用水路そばは蚊が多いこと、老オースティンが高熱を出していたことからマラリアが死因だという推測があります。このときジェインは29歳。生活の困窮によって執筆からますます遠ざかることになってしまいます。（次章コラムに続く）

Chapter 10

Get ready with vocabulary!

Match the Japanese words 1～10 with the English words given below.

1（脳卒中などの）発作　2 動転している　3 台なしにする
4 癇癪を起す　5 ばかげた　6 恐れる　7 気が進まない
8 心配している　9 動揺したようすで　10 確認する

dread	agitatedly	concerned	reluctant	confirm
seizure	ruin	upset	lose one's temper	absurd

Enjoy the story!

01 Catherine listened to Henry again

Answer the following questions in Japanese as you read the story.

1 What was the cause of Mrs. Tilney's death?
ティルニー夫人の死因は何だったのでしょう。

2 How many doctors were called in for Mrs. Tilney?
ティルニー夫人のため、何人の医者が呼ばれましたか。

3 How did Catherine feel when she was informed of the real circumstances of Mrs. Tilney's death? What did she say?
ティルニー夫人の死の状況を知らされてキャサリンはどう感じましたか。そしてどう言いましたか。

2-17

"My mother's illness was **seizure.** It led her to death. It was nine years ago. And I was with her when she expired." Now Catherine was turning pale. Henry Tilney continued, "On the third day, a doctor was called in. He stayed with her all day and night. On the fourth day, two more doctors were called in. She died on the fifth day. We did all we could do. Poor Eleanor was away from home. She couldn't be with her mother in her last moments."

"Then, then, your father was...."

"My father was **upset** for a long time after her death. If

you think he didn't love her, you're mistaken. He loved her very much. It is true he often **lost his temper** in front of her. But his feelings towards her was sincere and still haven't changed." ◆

Deeply embarrassed or almost frozen, Catherine could only say, "I'm glad to hear it."

"Miss Morland, please. What have you been imagining? Where did you get that idea?"

Catherine could not bear her shame anymore and ran away to her room.

02　A letter from James

Answer the following questions in Japanese as you read the story.

1 How did Henry Tilney act towards Catherine when she went down to apologize?

キャサリンが謝罪しようと階下に降りてきたとき、ヘンリー・ティルニーは彼女にどう接しましたか。

2 What led Catherine to the absurd idea about General Tilney, according to her self-analysis?

キャサリンの自己分析によれば、彼女はなぜティルニー将軍についてばかげた考えを抱くようになったのでしょう。

3 What news did the letter from James convey?

ジェイムズの手紙は何を知らせてきましたか。

She cried and cried till her tears dried. Henry Tilney now knew she had held such a terrible idea about his father. How could she ask him to forgive her? "I have **ruined** everything with him." She thought of the kindness that Henry and Eleanor, and General himself had shown to her. "I cannot stay with them. But I have to give my apologies before I go." Catherine finally went downstairs **dreading** what Henry would say to her.

Henry was waiting for her to come down. And he was more attentive to Catherine than ever. He seemed to have realized that Catherine never needed comfort more.

For a few days, she thought about "how she had gotten the idea" herself and now she knew that the **absurd** misunderstanding was the result of her over-active imagination under the influence of the novels she had been reading. Catherine became to forgive herself and Henry remained attentive to her.

Things were getting back to normal, and Henry and Catherine were closer than ever. Then, on the tenth morning of her stay at the Abbey, Catherine received a letter at the breakfast table. It was from her brother James. Catherine's face changed while reading it.

Dear Catherine,

*I'm **reluctant** to write this, but I must tell you that Miss Thorpe and I are not engaged anymore. Everything between us is over. I won't go into the details but soon you will hear more than you need to. I hope you will leave Northanger Abbey before Captain Tilney goes back there. What hurts is the fact that she lied to me. I still don't understand why. I wish we had never met. Be careful where you give your heart.*

Your brother, James

Catherine's eyes were filled with tears, which ran down her cheeks. Henry and Eleanor soon realized that it was not good news. Catherine left the table without a word.

03 Catherine comforts Eleanor and Henry

Answer the following questions in Japanese as you read the story.

1 What was the favour that Catherine asked of Henry and Eleanor?

キャサリンはヘンリーとエレノアに何をお願いしましたか。

2 What did Henry Tilney ask Catherine concerning the Thorpe family?

ヘンリー・ティルニーはソープ一家に関してキャサリンにどんなことを尋ねましたか。

3 Why do you think Henry and Eleanor looked at each other? Make a guess and state your reason to support it.

なぜヘンリーとエレノアは視線を交わしたのでしょう。推測して、根拠を述べましょう。

Half an hour later Catherine came down, for she was aware both Henry and Eleanor had looked very **concerned.**

"Something grave happened to your parents?" asked Eleanor.

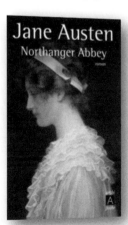

"No, my parents are well. It's my brother James. He is so unhappy, and you'll soon know why."

"But he is fortunate to have a sister like you, who cares for him so much," said Henry.

"I have a favour to ask," said Catherine **agitatedly.** "If Captain Tilney is coming here, please tell me so that I can leave."

"Our brother Frederick, you mean?" asked Eleanor.

"Yes. It will be difficult for me to be in the same room with him after what happened to my brother."

Henry guessed what had happened to the three in Bath. He

read the letter himself and his suspicions were **confirmed**. Catherine said, "Isabella has left my brother and is going to marry yours." But Henry thought it was unlikely. He asked, "Are the Thorpes very wealthy? Are they an old family with their country?"

Catherine told him what she knew. "I don't think so. Isabella said she had no money. But that doesn't matter to your family, does it? When I came here, General Tilney told me that he could not care less about money or family name."

Eleanor and Henry looked at each other.

Then Eleanor said, "But will Frederick be happy if he marries such a girl? She has left one person heartbroken to marry another so soon."

Henry added, "And I don't think Miss Thorpe left her fiancé before making sure that the next man is going to marry her. Poor Frederick."

Catherine was the one who comfort them this time. "She might behave better to your family than to mine. And once she is married to a man she really loves, she will be loyal to him."

"Yes, I'm afraid she will!" said Henry.

» Reviewing the story

Ⅰ ● Reorder a)～e) according to the story.

a) Henry Tilney remained attentive to Catherine and they became closer.

b) Henry, Eleanor, and Catherine talked about the possibility of Captain Tilney marrying Isabella Thorpe.

c) Henry Tilney explained to Catherine how his mother had died.

d) Catherine felt ashamed and ran away from Henry.

e) Catherine received a letter from James, which told that he had broken up with Isabella Thorpe.

Ⅱ ● Complete the sentences using the given words.

agitatedly	confirmed	absurd	dreaded	seizure

1 Mrs. Tilney died of [   ].

2 Catherine, who had [   ] Henry's reaction, was saved by his kindness.

3 Catherine reflected on how the [   ] idea about Mrs. Tilney had occurred to her.

4 Catherine [   ] asked Henry and Elanor to let her know in advance of Captain Tilney's homecoming.

5 The letter from James [   ] Henry's suspicions about Isabella and Frederick.

» Listening and oral practices

Fill the blanks as you listen and practice the conversation with your partners.

A：Are the Thorpes very wealthy? Are they a rich, old family?

B：I don't think so, for Isabella said she had no money. But [¹

]?

C：Why do you say so?

B：General Tilney told me that [²   ] or family name.

C：Oh.... But will Frederick be happy if he marries such a girl? [³

] to marry another so soon.

A：I guess Miss Thorpe left her fiancé after making sure [⁴

].

B：Maybe. But with your brother, I think she will behave herself.

A：I'm afraid she will.

» Tips for reading

疑問詞が導く名詞節

if（～かどうか）や that に加え、疑問詞 what, which, when, where, why, how も名詞節を導く。

What hurts is that she lied to me. 何が苦しいかというと、彼女が僕に嘘をついたことだ。

Be careful **where you give your heart**. どこに心を捧げるか気をつけなさい。

I don't know **how I can tell this**. これをどう伝えればいいのかわからないわ。（Chapter 11）

▶ 英語を完成しましょう。（日本文の下線部は英文の名詞節にあたる。）

1）Catherine had a romantic vision of [   ] from an abbey
should look like.　僧院を改装したカントリーハウスはどんなものか、キャサリンにはロマ
ンティックなイメージがあったのです。（Chapter 9）

2）Everybody has the right to do [   ].
皆、自分の（his）お金を好きなようにする権利があるわ。（Chapter 6）

3）James could not understand [   ] her mind so suddenly.
ジェイムズにはなぜ突然イザベラが心変わりしたかわからなかった。

4）Catherine told her parents [   ] towards her.
キャサリンは、自分に対しての気持ちを将軍が急に変えたこと（どう変えたか）を両親に
告げた。（Chapter 11）

5）Catherine is to be hurt to hear [   ] Northanger Abbey.
キャサリンは、いつどんなふうに自分がノーサンガー・アビーを去らねばならないかを聞
いて傷つくことになります。

81

注）名詞節の中で未来は未来形のまま、<u>副詞節</u>の中では未来は現在形。

Will Frederick be happy <u>if he marries such a girl</u>?

I'd like to leave Northanger Abbey <u>before Captain Tilney comes back</u>.

◀ 反語 ▶　How could～?　How can ～?　　しばしば反語的意味を持つ。

How could you come here?「よく（も）来れたものですね。」

= You are audacious/shameless/impudent to have come here.

　注）How did you come here? は交通手段等を尋ねている。

How could she ask him to forgive her ?　許してくれと頼めただろうか（いや、できはしない。）

Oh, **how can** I tell ?　(Chapter 11) 言えやしないわ。

▶ **英語を完成しましょう。**

1)　[　　　　　　　　　　　　　　　] such a thing to James?

　　イザベラはジェイムズにあんな仕打ちをよくできたものだね。

2)　We may well wonder, "[　　　　　　　　　　　　　　　　　] such a wild imagination?"

　　「キャサリンはよくあんなとんでもない想像ができるなぁ」と思うのも当然でしょう。

❯❯ Read a part of the original passage

Catherine had not read three lines before her sudden change of countenance, and short exclamations of sorrowing wonder, declared her to be receiving unpleasant news; and Henry, earnestly watching her through the whole letter, saw plainly that it ended no better than it began. He was prevented, however, from even looking his surprise by his father's entrance. They went to breakfast directly; but Catherine could hardly eat anything. Tears filled her eyes, and even ran down her cheeks as she sat.

❯❯ Write a passage as a character

A)　Write a passage of 3〜6 sentences from Catherine's diary reflecting what happened right after she had left Mrs. Tilney's bedroom.

B)　Or write a passage of 3〜5 sentences from Eleanor's diary written after she had read James' letter and remembered how Isabella had interrupted her conversation with Catherine in Bath before.

作者ジェイン・オースティンのこと（3）

サザンプトン

　1805 年バースで父を亡くしたジェイン。悲しみもさることながら、この突然の不幸でオースティン姉妹と母は経済的にもいよいよ窮地に陥ります。ウォリックシャーに領地とカントリーハウス、ストーンリー・アビーを所有する母方リー家の所有者が跡継ぎのないまま死去し、その財産の一部を相続すべく動きましたがうまくいきませんでした。（ただ訪れた大邸宅内部のようすは『説得』など後の作品に直接活かされています。）3 人はしばらくオースティン兄弟たちの不定期な援助を受けてしのいでいましたが、それは先の見えない辛い生活でした。執筆中だった小説 "The Watsons" は父の死を機に筆が止まり、結局完成していません。

サザンプトンのオールセインツ教会

　貧困から脱出する策として 3 人は、海軍で働く五男フランシスと末っ子のチャールズのいる軍港サザンプトンに移ることにします。この町は姉妹が子どものころ寄宿学校に入り、ジェインが 18 才のときに従姉を訪ねて滞在した町でもありました。軍務のためしばしば長期に留守をするフランシスの家で、彼の妊娠中の新妻と母と姉たちが協力して暮らすことは、つまるところ皆に好都合だったのです。さいわいにもこの借家には庭があり、野菜や花を植えることができました。

　サザンプトンは古代ローマ時代からの物流の拠点で、長くワイン貿易で栄え、後にはエリザベス一世の援助を受けたドレイク船長らがスペイン船やポルトガル船からの掠奪品を持ち帰った港であり、ジェインの時代においても重要な軍港でした。とはいえバースに比べれば薄汚れた印象の「格下」の町という印象はぬぐえません。また、家賃と食費は弟と母が出しましたが、その他はすべて姉妹、とくにジェインの肩にかかってきました。バースで出会って親しくなったリリントンという老婦人が 1806 年 1 月末、姉妹それぞれに 50 ポンドの小さな遺産を遺してくれたのですが、それもたちまち費えました。1807 年にジェインが書きとめた、その 50 ポンドの支出記録を見れば、洗濯代や薬、手紙と小荷物の郵送費に加え、ピアノのリース料と、また女中のチップと慈善に使ったことがわかります。ジェインの作品には常に音楽のシーンがあります。作品に登場する実在の作曲家は、同時代のクレイマー（Johann Baptist Cramer, 1771-1858）だけですが、牧師館時代はハプシコードかピアノを愛用していました。また『エマ（*Emma*）』の主人公は "Without music, my life will be blank" と言っています。さらにチップと慈善は合わせて 16 ポンドほど、つまり貰った額の 3 分の 1 ほどを占めます。音楽と、そして自分より困っている人に分け与えることはジェインの「必需品」だったようです。

　ジェインの新たな収入源は「書くこと」だけなのに、サザンプトン時代、ジェインにはその時間も場所もありませんでした。この町で母、姉、弟フランシスの妻とその妹、そして「もう一人の姉」とも慕ってきた友人のマーサ・ロイドと女中たちが身を寄せ合ってぎりぎりの生計を立てていました。総じて、1805 年に父を失ってからチョートンに移る 1809 年までの女性どうし肩寄せあって暮らした数年は、ジェインの人生の底辺と見ることができます。

チョートン・コテッジ、そしてロンドンで執筆

　1809 年、ケント州の遠戚ナイト家の養子となって
いた兄エドワードから援助の手が差しのべられます。
前年に妻を亡くしてようやく生家の身内のほうに心
が向いたのでしょうか。彼は故郷スティーブントン
村のあるハンプシャー州のチョートンにも邸宅と領
地をもっていました。エリザベス朝様式の邸宅チョー
トン・ハウスです。ただしジェインたちの住まいと
して提供されたのはその邸宅に付随する家屋、チョー
トン・コテッジでした。

チョートン・ハウス（エドワードが相続した
屋敷の一つ）

　ときにジェインは 33 才。この 17 世紀建造の建物で、
朝早く起床してピアノを弾き、午前 9 時に朝食の用意を
したあとはカッサンドラとマーサの協力で家事から解放
される、という日課となりました。スティーブントンを
離れて以来ようやく落ち着いた生活を取り戻したのです
。この家でジェインは、若いころ書き始めていた小説
を書き直して仕上げ、新たなストーリーを生み出し、堰
を切ったように作品を世に送り出しています。世間に知

チョートン・コテッジ（現ジェイン・オー
スティンズハウス博物館）

られないよう匿名で発表していたので、ドアの蝶番は軋
んで音がするよう油をささずにおき、訪問者から原稿を隠すための数秒を確保していました。
1811 年に『分別と多感（Sense and Sensibility）』、1813 年には『高慢と偏見（Pride and Preju-
dice）』、1814 年には『マンスフィールド・パーク（Mansfield Park）』、そして 1815 年には『エ
マ』を出版しています。彼女が執筆に使った小さなテーブルを見ると、このひっそりとした片
隅から次々と世界的な名作が生まれたことに感銘を禁じえません。不動の人気作家となる道が
見えていました。

　ジェインはまた兄ヘンリーのロンドンの家にも滞在しました。ヘン
リーも妻を亡くしており家を空けることが多かったので、庭があるこ
の家でジェインは伸び伸びと筆を走らせ、また兄の馬車に乗って出版
社との打ち合わせと交渉に出向きました。

　『高慢と偏見』は出版にこぎつけると予期せぬヒットとなり 140 ポン
ドの印税をもたらしました。出版社はしかしその 3 倍の利益を得てい
ます。そこでジェインは次の『マンスフィールド・パーク』では、出
版費用のリスクを負うが入る印税は高くなる、自費出版に近い形に変
えました。しかし残念ながら『高慢と偏見』ほどは売れませんでした。
結局、生前ジェインは全作品で、およそ 650 ポンドの印税を得るにと
どまっています。

チョートン・コテッジに
残るジェインの机

ウィンチェスターへ

　ようやく作家として手にした成功。安定した生活。しかしこの幸せは長くは続きませんで
した。ジェインは 1816 年の 7 月、脱力感と疲労感を自覚しはじめ、数週間後には、背中に激
しい痛みを感じたと書きとめています。実は、早くからジェインの作品の出版に奔走してくれ
た兄ヘンリーが少し前に破産しており、それが精神的な痛手ともなっていました。容態がまし
な時期もありましたが、12 月 16 日、ジェインは「歩けないのでパーティへの招待を断らざる

を得ない」ことを書き知らせています。

　年が変わって 1817 年、4 月 6 日の手紙には、「2 週間ずっと具合が悪く、絶対に書く必要のあるものでなければ何も書けない "I have been really too unwell the last fortnight to write anything that was not absolutely necessary"」と弟のチャールズに書き送り、5 月 22 日には友人のアン・シャープへの手紙で「発熱と脱力感」を訴え、「高名なライフォード医師（Mr. Lyford）の治療を受けるため、姉とウィンチェスターへ移住する」と報告しています。チョートンを去る直前に見舞った姪のキャロライン・オースティン（ジェイムズの娘）は叔母ジェインのことを、「青ざめた顔で座って低い弱々しい声で話していた」と書きとめています。

ウィンチェスターでジェインが滞在した家　©Peter Trimming

　ジェインは自分の病気を「＜胆汁＞のしわざ」ではないかと疑っていました。しかし背中の痛みに加え、膝の痛み、発熱、消化器の不調、下痢、脱力、意識障害といった症状の記録から、今ではアジソン病、あるいは全身性エリテマトーデスだったと推察され、ジェインが手紙に残した容体の描写はこれら難病の症状の最初の詳細な記録と見られています。

　『ノーサンガー・アビー』は、こんな状態のなかで推敲され、仕上げられて、そして作者の死後、兄ヘンリーによって出版されました。そのとき初めてジェインの名前が作品に付記されました。本書まえがきで触れましたが、魂の叫びで読者を魅了し続ける女性作家の作品としては、たとえば少し後のエミリー・ブロンテ作『嵐が丘』が知られるところでしょう。しかしジェインによるこの「軽い玉の輿物語」や『説得』も実のところ、死が間近に迫るなか、尋常でない忍耐と鬼気迫る創作意欲によって完成された物語だったのです。

　ウィンチェスターに借りた質素なアパートが、ジェインの最後の住処となりました。付き添っていた姉カッサンドラは、ジェインの最期、1817 年 7 月 18 日のようすを、その 2 日後にジェインのお気に入りの姪ファニーへ宛てた手紙でこう書き送っています。悲しみを抑えて愛する妹の死を綴る、静かに心打つ文章を読んでみましょう。

"On Thursday I went into the town to do an errand your dear Aunt was anxious about. I returned about a quarter before six & found her recovering from faintness and oppression, she got so well as to be able to give me a minute account of her seizure and when the clock struck 6 she was talking quietly to me. I cannot say how soon afterwards she was seized again with the same faintness, which was followed by sufferings she could not describe, but Mr. Lyford had been sent for, had applied something to give her ease & she was in a state of quiet insensibility by seven at the latest. From that time till half past four, when she ceased to breathe, she scarcely moved a limb."

ウィンチェスター大聖堂

　当時女性は葬列に加わらないためカッサンドラは窓から妹を見送り、ヘンリーとエドワードとフランシス、そして病床にあったジェイムズに代って息子ジェイムズ＝エドワードが棺に付き添いました。

　ジェインの遺体はウィンチェスター大聖堂に葬られました。破産後に牧師補となっていた兄ヘンリーの尽力があったとされます。大聖堂の床の墓碑銘に小説家としてのジェインへの言及はなく、彼女の死

から半世紀以上経た 1870 年、棺に付き添った甥ジェイムズ＝エドワードが、ジェイン伝を書いて得た印税で大聖堂の壁に真鍮板の墓碑銘を設えました。しかしここにも、「その著作よって多くに知られる "Known to many by her writings"」とあるだけです。墓碑銘の最後には「箴言」からの引用 "She opened her mouth with wisdom and in her tongue is the law of kindness" (31:26) と刻まれていますが、ジェインの読者なら、"and the law of irony and humour" と加えたいところですね。今、ウィンチェスター大聖堂は、バースやチョートンの住居と並んで、世界中のファンがジェイン・オースティンを偲ぶ聖地となっています。

さて近年、ジェインの作品だけでなく、ジェイン自身の恋や作家への道を描く伝記的な映画が制作されています。一方、ジェインの死後カッサンドラと兄ヘンリーがジェインの残した手紙の大部分、約 3000 通を焼却処分していることから、『レディ・スーザン』のような辛辣な書簡体小説が失われた可能性もあり、稀代のリアリスト作家の全貌は永遠に失われたのかもしれません。しかし今に残る作品 6 篇については心理学の視点からセリフを分析したり、entail と呼ばれるイングランドの相続慣習と相続法に照らして人物の関係

ジェイン・オースティンが居住、滞在、訪問した町や村

を見直したり、あらゆる研究がなされ、わが国でも優れた研究書や翻訳が出版されてきました。教室で皆さんを導いてくださる先生も専門家のお一人かもしれません。ジェインの作品や時代背景についてさらに尋ねてみてはいかがでしょう。またサザンプトンは第二次世界大戦の爆撃によって様変わりしましたが、バースやライム・リージスにはジェインの時代の建物の多くがほぼそのまま残っています。まずは Google 地図で訪れてみましょう。

コラム 8〜10　作者ジェイン・オースティンのこと（1）〜（3）　参考資料

Jane Austen's Letters（https://www.gutenberg.org/ebooks/42078）

Jane Austen: Her Life by Park Honan（Weidenfeld & Nicolson; New: 1988）

Jane Austen Country（A documentary film directed by Liam Dale, produced by Wolfgang Fetten and Michelle Justice, Cobra Entertainment in 2002）

Jane Austen's footsteps（https://historicsouthampton.co.uk/austen/）2019 年 5 月 12 日取得

Lady Susan: Missing Masterpiece by Jane Austen（A Documentary film directed and produced by Michelle Lambeau, with Jane Austen House Museum, Phoenix Art Museum in 2013）

Chapter

11

Chapter 11

NORTHANGER ABBEY

» Get Ready with vocabulary!

Match the Japanese words 1〜10 with the English words given below.

1 終結　　2 緊張している　　　3 用事・約束　　4 惨めな

5 目撃する　　6 舞い上がっている　　7 かなりの　　8 相続する

9 敷地（と地位）　　10 子爵（伯爵、侯爵、公爵の嫡子）

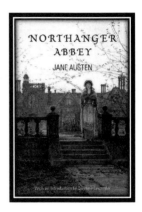

> viscount　　termination　　inherit　　engagement　　witness
>
> elated　　substantial　　nervous　　estate　　miserable

» Enjoy the story!

01 Catherine leaves Northanger Abbey

Answer the following questions in Japanese as you read the story.

1 What did Catherine understand anew about Isabella?

キャサリンはイザベラについて何をあらためて理解したでしょう。

2 Why was Catherine nervous when a carriage arrived at Northanger Abbey?

馬車がノーサンガー・アビーに到着したときキャサリンはなぜ緊張したのですか。

3 What did Eleanor worry about concerning Catherine's journey back to Fullerton?

キャサリンのフラトンへの帰路について、エレノアは何を心配しましたか。

　　Catherine, for the first time, began to suspect that marriage was all about money and ambition for Isabella. Though she was upset that she had lost one of her closest friends, she did not miss her. She spent the next few days peacefully with Eleanor, expecting James would soon grow out of the sad **termination** of his romance. Catherine also visited Henry in Woodston with Eleanor and found his place warm and comfortable.

　　Now Catherine's only worry was that she might be overstaying their welcome at the Abbey. Catherine told so to Eleanor, but Eleanor insisted that Catherine should stay at least another three weeks. They were now such good friends that they knew they would miss each other when separated. ◆

　　One evening, after they had drawn back to their rooms, a carriage came up to the Abbey. Catherine thought that it was Captain Frederick Tilney and felt a little **nervous**. About a quarter of an hour later, Eleanor knocked at her door.

"Catherine, I'm so sorry. I don't know how I can tell this. Oh, how can I tell?" Eleanor was awfully upset.

"Was the carriage Captain Frederick's?"

"No, it was my father. And, and... he requests you to leave here tomorrow." Eleanor hesitated but continued, "He remembered that he and I have an **engagement** on Monday and we must go. So, you need to leave here early tomorrow morning. What worries me is that you must go without a servant, as my father has decided so, and it is such a long way for a young woman to go alone."

"Oh my, is it because I have done something to offend your father?"

"I can't think of anything you've done and likely to have offended him. But he is in a very bad temper. I couldn't even ask the reason."

02 Catherine comes back to Fullerton

Answer the following questions in Japanese as you read the story.

1 The change in the General's feelings towards Catherine did not matter to Mr. and Mrs. Morland. Why not?

キャサリンに対する将軍の気持ちの変化がモーランド夫妻にとって大したことでなかったのはなぜでしょう。

2 What advice did Mrs. Morland give to Catherine?

モーランド夫人はキャサリンにどんな忠告をしましたか。

3 What was Catherine thinking of while walking around the village?

村を歩き回りながら、キャサリンはどんなことを想っていたでしょう。

The driver of the carriage knew where to take Catherine. She was too **miserable** to notice much about the long journey.

Her family, on the other hand, was very pleased to see her. She had been away for more than ten weeks. She was too sad to talk about Henry. She let them know how General Tilney's feelings had suddenly changed towards her and that she could not understand why. Her parents could not understand it, either. But they decided that it was not worth worrying about since Catherine had safely returned to Fullerton.

Catherine missed Eleanor and felt she had left half of herself at Northanger Abbey. "What did Henry think and say to find I was not there." For the next several days she could not sit still for more than ten minutes. Though her mother told her, "Try to be useful", she could not concentrate on anything.

She just walked around the village because she could not forget about Henry Tilney. The smile he showed when she went down to apologize, his look of satisfaction when she said she wanted to dance with him at the Ball Room, and…. Then, coming back home from a walk, she was told there was a visitor for her.

03 Catherine returns to Northanger Abbey

Answer the following questions in Japanese as you read the story.

1 Why did General Tilney invite Catherine to stay at Northanger Abbey in the first place?

ティルニー将軍はそもそもなぜキャサリンをノーサンガー・アビーに招いたのですか。

2 Why did General Tilney throw Catherine out of Northanger Abbey?

ティルニー将軍はなぜキャサリンをノーサンガー・アビーから追い出したのですか。

3 Why did General Tilney give Henry a reluctant permission to marry Catherine Morland?

ティルニー将軍が、気が進まずともヘンリーにキャサリンとの結婚を許可したのはなぜでしょう。

(2-23)

It was Henry Tilney. First, he apologized to Catherine for what his father had done to her. Then he asked her if they could speak privately.

Mr. and Mrs. Morland's surprise was considerable.

He explained that she was not to blame for anything. It was just that General Tilney had been led to believe Catherine was much richer than she really was.

When the General **witnessed** Henry paying special attention to Catherine at the dance in Bath, he asked John Thorpe about her, for the General had seen John talk to Catherine before that.

John Thorpe was too proud and **elated** to be spoken to by such an important person as the General. Since he himself was planning to marry Catherine at the time, he could not contain himself and boasted more than usual. He described Morland family as much wealthier than they really were. He even told that Catherine was an heiress of some large properties in Fullerton. General Tilney invited her to his house believing that she would bring a **substantial** amount of money as dowry to his son, and in some time, would **inherit** those properties.

After Catherine had rejected John and Isabella had broken up with James, the General by chance met John again. John Thorpe this time told the General that Mr. Morland had too many children and he would not be able to provide for his sons and daughters. He said to the General, "In short, sir, they are good for nothing."

Thus, as soon as the General returned to the Abbey, he threw Catherine out.

Catherine, to be honest, felt a secret satisfaction to know these things, for they proved cruelty she had suspected in the General. As for Henry, he told his father that he was going to ask Catherine Morland to marry him whatever her family was like.

Then soon the General left Henry to do as he liked, saying "Be a fool. Do whatever you like". It was mainly because Eleanor became engaged with an extremely rich man. She had been in love for some time with this gentleman, and recently he inherited a vast fortune with the title of **viscount** rather unexpectedly. So, Eleanor will soon become a viscountess with her own **estate**. Frederick, with

no intention to marry Isabella Thorpe as everybody knew except for herself, soon left England for his military duty.

"So, Miss Morland, will you marry me?" proposed Henry.

~~~

Now Mr. Henry Tilney and Mrs. Catherine M. Tilney live at Northanger Abbey with its history and legends. As our readers wisely imagine, Mrs. Tilney never stopped reading novels.

The End

» Reviewing the story

Ⅰ ● Reorder a) ~ e) according to the story.

a) Henry Tilney visited Catherine in Fullerton and apologized to her about his father's rudeness.

b) Henry Tilney explained why his father invited Catherine to the Abbey in the first place and threw her out later.

c) General Tilney came back to Northanger Abbey and immediately sent Catherine back to Fullerton.

d) Catherine, unable to forget Henry Tilney, walked around the village.

e) Catherine made a long journey home without any attendant.

II ● Complete the sentences using the given words.

| inherit | elated | substantial | nervous | witnessed |

1 James' letter made Catherine [   ] and afraid of seeing Captain Tilney.

2 Having [   ] his son paying a special attention to Catherine, General Tilney sought for information on her family.

3 John Thorpe was [   ] to be talked to by the General.

4 John Thorpe boasted that Catherine would [   ] some properties in Fullerton.

5 General Tilney expected Catherine to bring a [   ] amount of dowry to the Tilney family.

》 Listening and oral practices

Fill the blanks as you listen and practice the conversation with your partner.   (2-24)

A : Catherine, I'm sorry, [1   ]. Oh, how can I tell?

B : Was the carriage Captain Frederick's?

A : No, it was my father. And... [2   ].

B : Tomorrow? So soon.

A : He remembered we have an engagement on Monday. [3   ] that you must go without a servant to attend you. It is such a long way for a young woman to go alone.

B : Oh, my, is it because [4   ]?

A : I can't think of anything of that kind.

》 Tips for reading

◀ than のあとの「先行詞＋関係詞」の省略 ▶

General Tilney had believed Catherine was much richer **than** (a girl who / what) she really was.

John described Morland family as much wealthier **than** (a family which / what) they really were.

▶ 日本語に訳しましょう。

For Isabella, marriage was nothing more than money and ambition meant.

[   ]

◀ whatever / whichever / who (m) ever が導く副詞節・名詞節 ▶
◀ whenever / wherever / however が導く副詞節 ▶

Henry told his father that he was going to ask Catherine to marry him **whatever her family was like**. 彼女の家族がどんなのであろうとも―副詞節

The General told Henry, "Be a fool. Do **whatever you like**." 何でも好きなことを―名詞節

▶ 英語を完成しましょう。

1) [   ], she would make her partner unhappy.

フレデリックとジェイムズのどちらと結婚しようがイザベラは相手を不幸にするだろう。

2) [   ] should understand her pleasure of reading.

キャサリンと結婚する人は誰であれ、彼女の読書の喜びを理解してしかるべきだ。

▶ 日本語に直しましょう。

3) However generous and understanding Henry may be, he would not change his own idea of how a couple should be. [   ]

4) Captain Tilney cannot care less about whatever become of his "girlfriends".

[   ]

» Read a part of the original passage

Her (Eleanor's) partiality for this gentleman was not of recent origin; and he had been long withheld only by inferiority of situation from addressing her. His unexpected accession to title and fortune had removed all his difficulties. (...) The influence of the viscount and viscountess in their brother's behalf was assisted by that right understanding of Mr. Morland's circumstances which, as soon as the general would allow himself to be informed, they were qualified to give. It taught him that he had been scarcely more misled by Thorpe's first boast of the family wealth than by his subsequent malicious overthrow of it; that in no sense of the word were they necessitous or poor, and that Catherine would have three thousand pounds. (...) Henry and Catherine were married, the bells rang, and everybody smiled; and, as this took place within a twelve month from the first day of their meeting, it will not appear, after all the dreadful delays occasioned by the general's cruelty, that they were essentially hurt by it. To begin perfect happiness at the respective ages of twenty-six and eighteen is to do pretty well; (...) by improving their knowledge of each other, and adding strength to their attachment, I leave it to be settled, by whomsoever it may concern, whether the tendency of this work be altogether to recommend parental tyranny, or reward filial disobedience.

» Write a passage as a character

Write a letter of 5～7 sentences that Mrs. Morland wrote to James about Catherine's homecoming and engagement.

読書の愉しみ "There is no enjoyment like reading!"

　ジェイン・オースティンは『ノーサンガー・アビー』で、小説に夢中になって現実が見えなくなっているキャサリンに少しお灸をすえています。しかし当然ながら、小説など虚構の物語そのものを否定しているわけではありません。批判は、虚構と現実の区別がつかないことに向けられているのです。別のジェインの小説『エマ』では主人公エマが独りよがりな「善意」でカップルを成立させようとしますが、ジェインはそんなエマについて "She will never submit to anything requiring industry and patience and a subjection of the fancy to the understanding." と、相手役のナイトリーの口を借りて厳しくコメントしています。キャサリンとエマが夫となる男性の導きによってその欠点を乗り越えるという設定には違和感が残りますが、それはさておきジェイン自身、キャサリンが愛読したアン・ラドクリフの恐怖小説も楽しんでいたことがわかっています。ただしキャサリンと異なりジェインの読書の幅は広く、子供時代から歴史書になじみ、同時代のマライア・エッジワースや少し前のファーニー・バーニー、大御所評論家のサミュエル・ジョンソン、さらにレディング寄宿学校では『若きウェルテルの悩み』の英訳を読んでいた記録があります。そしてキャサリンのお相手ヘンリー・ティルニーに、"The person, be it gentleman or lady, who has not pleasure in a good novel, must be intolerably stupid." と読書の愉しみを擁護するセリフを与えています。ヘンリーはキャサリンと読書の喜びを共有していける人なのでしょう。

　ところで2017年、国民的人気作家ジェイン・オースティンの没後200年を記念し、その肖像が10ポンド紙幣となりました。10ポンドは奇しくも、ジェインが『ノーサンガー・アビー』の原型とされる『レディ・スーザン』の原稿を出版社に売り、のちに買い戻した金額です。そして紙幣のジェインの肖像の下には、"I declare after all there is no enjoyment like reading!"「結局、読書ほど楽しいことはないと言い切れるわ」とジェインの小説からの引用があります。ただしこれは、ジェインの代表作『高慢と偏見』に登場する浅はかで嫌な人物キャロライン・ビングリーのセリフです。自分の意中の男性ダーシーが「（女性には）幅広い読書によって心を向上させてほしい」と言うのを聞き、即座に読書好きを装って吐いたセリフなのです。ジェインの小説のなかの数ある名セリフのなかからこれを紙幣に印刷するとは、いかにもイギリスらしい、そしてジェインの本質を踏まえた捻りのある選択ですね。

　本書の学習を終えた皆さんは、ぜひ『ノーサンガー・アビー』の原作を読んでください。結論が分かっていても、漱石が言う「写実の泰斗」と「技神」を味わってニンマリハラハラ、「読書の愉しみ」を実感されることでしょう。われらがキャサリン・モーランドも、この尽きぬ愉しみのゆえ、世の現実を知ってからもやはり小説を読み続けるのです。

参考資料

"The Significance of Books and of Reading in Jane Austen's Novels" Lauren Gilbert (March 19, 2017) posted for *Austen Authors* (https://austenauthors.net/the-significance-of-books-and-of-reading-in-jane-austens-novels-a-guest-post-from-lauren-gilbert/)

» Exit Questions

I ● Complete the character descriptions 1~10 with the names below.

> Mrs. Allen / General Tilney / Isabella Thorpe / Eleanor Tilney
>
> Mr. Allen / Henry Tilney / John Thorpe / Catherine Morland
>
> James Morland / Captain Frederick Tilney

1 [   ] becomes the love interest of Isabella Thorpe, the younger sister to his friend John. He and Isabella become engaged but they break up because of her dishonesty.

2 [   ] is Catherine's romantic interest from the beginning of the story, and soon comes to return her feelings. He speaks with a little sarcasm but has a kind nature, which leads him to take a liking to Catherine's straightforward sincerity.

3 [   ] is a boastful young man with a rough manner, who certainly appears unpleasant to Catherine or anyone except for his family. He is rude to many people including his friends and family.

4 [   ] is a naive person who sees her life as if she was a heroine in a Gothic novel. She sees the best in people and is ignorant of other people's malicious intentions. However, she grows up through the experiences she has in Bath and at Northanger Abbey.

5 [   ] is a self-serving young woman on a quest to get a rich husband. Upon her arrival in Bath she immediately forms a quick friendship with Catherine Morland. She goes to every length to ensure a connection between her own family and the Morland family.

6 [   ] plays little part in Bath but takes on more importance back in Northanger Abbey. She likes Catherine and forms friendships with her. She is an obedient daughter, warm friend, sweet sister and becomes engaged to the man she loves when he inherits a noble title and estate.

7 [   ] holds an important position in the army. He is handsome and enjoys pursuing flirtations with pretty girls who are willing to offer him some encouragement.

8 [   ] is a kind, wealthy man who possesses many properties in Fullerton.

9 [   ] is fond of Catherine and a little vacuous person with interest in clothes above all.

10 [   ] is a military figure, probably retired, who plans to marry his son only to a

woman with substantial wealth. He has lost his wife nine years before the beginning of the story.

II • Reorder the passages A~K according to the story of *Northanger Abbey*. (The first is A and the last is K.)

Answer : 1-A   2   3   4   5   6   7   8   9   10   11-K

1 A
Seventeen-year-old Catherine Morland is one of the ten children of a well-off but not so rich family in Fullerton. She is very fond of reading Gothic novels, especially the works by Mrs. Ann Radcliffe. One day, Catherine is invited by the Allens, her wealthier neighbours, to accompany them and stay in Bath, a town popular for its socializing activities.

B   One night, in Henry's absence, the General returns to Northanger Abbey in a bad temper. He makes Eleanor tell Catherine that the family has an engagement which prevents Catherine from staying any longer. Thus, Catherine was put on the way back home early in the next morning without even a servant to see to her safety.

C   James and John arrive unexpectedly in Bath. While Isabella and James spend time together, Catherine becomes acquainted with John. But she finds him not so pleasant nor polite. Henry Tilney then returns to Bath, this time with his younger sister Eleanor, who is kind as well as sophisticated. Catherine also meets their father, General Tilney, who somehow pays attention to Catherine.

D   Catherine comes to think that her over-active imagination under the influence of those Gothic novels led her to act unreasonably. Henry lets her get over her shameful thoughts in her own time and stays attentive to her. Soon, James writes to inform Catherine that he has broken off his engagement to Isabella. His letter suggests that Isabella has become engaged, instead, to Captain Tilney. Henry and Eleanor, however, doubt that their brother has become engaged to Isabella Thorpe who has little money. Catherine is terribly disappointed, realising that for Isabella, marriage is not a matter of love but of ambition. Catherine passes several days with Henry and Eleanor at Northanger Abbey while General Tilney is away.

E   In Bath, Mrs. Allen and Catherine at first feel uncomfortable not to find any acquaintance. But soon Catherine is introduced to a pleasant young gentleman, Henry Tilney. She enjoys dancing and talking with him. Much to Catherine's disappointment, however, Henry does not appear in the following few days. Instead, she meets Isabella Thorpe, a flirtatious young woman. She is a daughter of Mrs. Thorpe, an old friend of Mrs. Allen's. Isabella and Catherine quickly become close. Catherine comes to know that Mrs Thorpe's son John is a friend of her own older brother, James.

F   At home, her parents are glad to have Catherine safely back. But Catherine is unhappy and cannot concentrate on anything. Two days after she returns home, however, Henry pays her an unexpected visit and explains what happened. General Tilney, believing John Thorpe's empty boasts, had thought Catherine to be a rich heiress, and therefore a proper match for Henry. Later in London, General Tilney ran into John Thorpe again. John, angry at Catherine's refusal of his half-made proposal of marriage, said this time that she was from a poor family.

G   Meanwhile, Isabella and James become engaged. James' father approves of their marriage and offers his son a living of the sum of 400 pounds annually. However, they must wait for two years till their marriage as well as the provision of the money. Isabella is not satisfied with the sum but pretends to be concerned about James, not herself. John suggests he also wants to marry Catherine while she has no such an intension. Soon Isabella begins to flirt with Captain Tilney, Henry's brother. Catherine cannot understand Isabella's behaviour. Henry on the other hand seems to understand all too well, as he knows his brother's character.

H   Catherine sneaks to one of Mrs. Tilney's rooms, only to find nothing strange or mysterious there. Unfortunately, Henry joins her in the corridor and asks why she is there. He guesses her inferences to Gothic novels, so informs her that his father loved his wife in his own way. Feeling ashamed, Catherine goes back to her room. Through her reflections on what has happened she realizes she has had too much of a wrong kind of imagination. She thinks she has ruined everything with Henry.

I   John Thorpe continuously tries to get in the way of Catherine's relationship with the Tilneys by imposing dances and country ridings. One day Catherine goes out on riding with John to see an old castle in spite that she has promised to go for a walk with Henry and Eleanor. This puts Catherine in the awkward position of having to explain her behaviour to Henry at the theatre soon later. Henry, however, seems to like her sincerity and candidness unintentionally shown in her desperate explanation of the situation.

J   Soon General Tilney invites Catherine to stay at their home, Northanger Abbey, for a few weeks. Catherine expects the place to have a foreboding and frightening atmosphere as the old castles that appear in her favourite novels. But to her disappointment, Northanger Abbey turns out to be a pleasant, orderly place. However, the house includes a mysterious part that

Catherine is not allowed to enter. General Tilney, who sounded rather cold, does not want Catherine to see the part. They used to be the rooms of Mrs. Tilney's who died nine years earlier. Catherine comes to know that Eleanor was not with her mother when her mother died. Catherine, with her wild imagination, concludes that General Tilney has imprisoned his wife somewhere in the house, if he has not murdered her like the villain in her favourite novel by Mrs. Radcliffe.

11 K   General Tilney had been given wrong information by John Thorpe again — this time, "the Morland family are poor and good for nothing". The General got furious and returned home to throw out Catherine. When Henry returned to Northanger Abbey from his own house in Woodston, he learned how Catherine had been thrown out. So he broke with his father and came to see her. — After having thus explained, Henry tells Catherine he wants to marry her. Catherine, of course, accepts his proposal. Eventually, General Tilney allows them to marry, though reluctantly. It is because Eleanor has now become engaged to a wealthy and titled man. Catherine starts her new life in Northanger Abbey with Henry and keeps enjoying novels.

Appendix Listening for chapter introduction

まず、I～XI それぞれの 1～4 の日本語に相当する英語を予測し、それから英語を聴いて側注欄等の余白に書きとりましょう。

I

Catherine Morland [1   ]. No one who had ever seen Catherine in her childhood would have thought that she was born to be a heroine. The Morlands were a family of ten children, and a family of ten children will always be called a fine family when there are heads and arms and legs enough for the number. But the Morlands were a [2   ]. They happily lived in the village of Fullerton.

At the age of seventeen, Catherine had never been in love, and no one had ever been in love with Catherine, either. Besides, in Fullerton, there were no eligible men. Lately, she was rather [3   ].

There lived, however, Mr. and Mrs. Allen, [4   ] in the village. Mr. Allen was not well and Mrs. Allen was fond of Catherine.

1 全く特別ではありませんでした

2 平凡な一家で、裕福でも貧しくもありません

3 小説を読むのに夢中

4 多くの不動産を所有していました

II

Catherine spent a lot of time with Isabella. They visited [1   ] in Bath arm in arm. When the weather was [2   ], they read novels together. They spoke about the novel Catherine was reading. It was *The Mystery of Udolpho* and Catherine was [3   ] of the story. Isabella said that she had already read the novel. "But I [4   ]," she added.

1 おしゃれな通りにあるおしゃれな店々
2 散歩に向いていない

3 まさにワクワクするところ
4 次に何が起こるか言わないわ

III

Soon there was a pleasant surprise: Mr. Tilney arrived. He looked dashing. He was talking to a young lady who was [1   ]. Catherine guessed right away that the lady was his sister.

The two came walking near Catherine. He recognized her and smiled. She smiled back and they came over to her. He explained that he had left Bath for a week [2   ] Catherine. He asked her for a dance, but Catherine did not accept because she [3   ] John Thorpe, who, unexpectedly, returned this moment.

When Catherine started to dance with John, however, he did not apologize for having kept her waiting. And she [4   ] during the dance. It was all about dogs and horses.

1 とても優雅でおしゃれな装いで

2 出会った直後に

3 といっしょに踊る約束をしていた

4 会話を嬉しく思っていませんでした

IV

Catherine came back to Allen's lodging at about three in the afternoon.

"How was your excursion?" asked Mrs. Allen.

"Very nice, thank you. [1   ]?" asked Catherine.

1 楽しい日だった

"Yes, I went to the Pump Room today. I saw Mrs. Thorpe there. She was glad that you went out with her son today."

"Who else did you see?" Catherine [2   ].

2 いくぶん探るように尋ねた

"I saw Mr. and Miss Tilney. I talked with them for quite some time and learned a lot about them. Mr. Tilney is a clergyman. I think they are [3   ]. They come from Gloucestershire."

3 いい人たちでとても裕福

Now Catherine was listening very attentively. "Yes? Which part of Gloucestershire?"

"I asked, but I forgot. Anyway, their mother, Mrs. Tilney, was Miss Drummond before her marriage. Her father gave her [4   ] and five hundred pounds for her wedding clothes. Of course, this was not the topic we talked about with Mr. and Miss Tilney."

4 二万ポンドの持参金

V

When the music stopped, Catherine [1   ]. He [2   ]. Then Henry excused himself and went to talk with him. The gentleman was still looking at Catherine while they were talking. She became very self-conscious and felt a little uneasy. Henry came back and said to her, "The gentleman was asking your name. So, you have the right to know his. He is General Tilney, my father." Catherine said, "Oh," with a great interest.

1 ひとりの年配の紳士が自分を見つめているのに気づいた
2 どちらかと言えば険しいが端正な顔立ちでもある

That evening, she had [3   ] with Eleanor Tilney. They talked about the beautiful scenery of the country around Bath. Eleanor invited Catherine to walk with her brother and herself the next day. "I'll call for you at twelve o'clock tomorrow, [4   ]" Catherine gladly agreed.

3 もう一度お喋りをする機会を

4 もし不都合でないなら

VI

"Oh, Catherine! Your brother is a wonderful person. I'm so happy!"

"What happened?" asked Catherine. Isabella said, "I only wish I will [1   ]." Catherine slowly began to understand what her news was. "Yes, Catherine. James proposed to me and [2   ]. He is on his way to Fullerton to ask your parents for their consent. You will be of our help, won't you?" Catherine nodded and Isabella continued, "We have so little money. Your parents may not like it. But we'll know everything tomorrow. Oh,

1 妻として彼の期待に沿う
2 彼の求婚を受け入れた

I can't wait!"

Catherine spent a couple of days [3   ]. Two days later, a
letter arrived from James announcing good news:

My dearest Isabella,

    [4   ]. *They kindly promised to do all they can do to help us
in our happiness.*

with all my love,
James Morland

3 ハラハラしている
  友人を励ました

4 両親は僕らが結婚
  するのに賛成して
  くれたよ

VII

Mr. and Mrs. Allen had been in Bath for six weeks and now they were
considering going back to Fullerton. Catherine wanted to stay in Bath and
continue to see Henry Tilney. [1   ] with Isabella, Catherine
wished she also would be [2   ]. Then the Allens decided to stay
in Bath for another three weeks. Catherine felt relieved.

But soon, Catherine was to leave Bath without the Allens, and it happened
like this.

One day, Eleanor Tilney informed Catherine that her father had decided
to leave Bath [3   ] with his family. Catherine could not
[4   ]. Then at the dance that evening, General Tilney himself
invited Catherine to their country house.

1 今や兄のジェイム
  ズが婚約したので
2 同類の出来事で祝
  福されたい

3 週の終わりに

4 失望を隠す

VIII

When Catherine finally arrived at Northanger Abbey, she found the place
[1   ] as she had expected. Rather, it was light and orderly with
large windows.

She was shown to her room and [2   ]. The room looked
comfortable and clean. As soon as she was alone, however, she began to
examine each corner of it looking for a secret door. She could not find any.

Soon Eleanor came to take her to the dinner table, where General Tilney
and Henry were waiting. Though [3   ], Henry and Eleanor
were very quiet when the General was with them. [4   ] was a
little restrained despite the kindness and consideration the Tilneys showed to
her.

1 それほど暗くも不
  気味でもない

2 晩餐の着替えのた
  めにひとりになっ
  た

3 何事もなく晩餐は
  進んだ
4 食卓での雰囲気

IX

About an hour later, while Catherine was resting, a maid came up to her room. She notified that the General was going to [1   ] with Eleanor around the Abbey for Catherine.

The General took Catherine through room after room and [2   ] on the furniture and the carpets, the paintings and the sculptures, and the fabrics and the draperies.

It is true that Catherine was [3   ] and the gardens. However, she was a little disappointed, because there were no secret rooms and passages to see. Catherine had a romantic vision of what [4   ]. The rather modern, orderly taste of the interior did not meet this vision of hers.

1 案内をする

2 彼女に詳しいことを教えた

3 外観に負けぬほど内装にも感心した

4 僧院を転用したカントリーハウスはかく見えるべきと

X

"My mother's illness was seizure. [1   ]. It was nine years ago. And I was with her when she expired." Now Catherine was turning pale. Henry Tilney continued, "On the third day, a doctor was called in. He stayed with her all day and night. On the fourth day, two more doctors were called in. She died on the fifth day. [2   ]. Poor Eleanor was away from home. She couldn't be with her mother in her last moments."

"Then, then, your father was...."

"My father was upset for a long time after her death. If you think he didn't love her, [3   ]. He loved her very much. It is true [4   ] in front of her. But his feelings towards her was sincere and still haven't changed.

1 母はそのせいで死んだ

2 われわれにできることは全てした

3 君は間違っている

4 彼はしばしば癇癪を起した

XI

Catherine, for the first time, began to suspect that [1   ] for Isabella. Though she was upset that she had lost one of her closest friends, she did not miss her. She spent the next few days peacefully with Eleanor, expecting James would soon [2   ]. Catherine also visited Henry in Woodston with Eleanor and found his place warm and comfortable.

Now Catherine's only worry was that [3   ] at the Abbey. Catherine told so to Eleanor, but Eleanor insisted that Catherine should stay at least another three weeks. They were now such good friends that they knew they would [4   ].

1 結婚とは金と野心のことである

2 自分のロマンスの悲しい終わり（の影響）を脱する

3 歓迎に甘えて長居しすぎる

4 離れるとお互いが居なくてさみしい

Chapter 1

- *Northanger Abbey* ジョン・ジョーンズ監督映画 2007 年ブラジル発売ポルトガル語版 DVD パッケージ
- *Northanger Abbey* Blackcat Publisher 2014 版 表紙 部分 ©Nadia Maestri（art director）
- *Northanger Abbey* Amazon audiobook 2007 表紙
- "Introduced... as Mr. Henry Tilney" *Northanger Abbey* 1907 年 版 H. M. Brock による挿絵
- Pump Room, the façade on Abbey Church Yard 筆者撮影
- "Catherine and Isabella arm in arm" *Northanger Abbey* 1904 版 H. M. Brock による挿絵
- *Northanger Abbey* ジョン・ジョーンズ監督映画 2007 年北米発売 DVD パッケージ
- *Captain William Wade, the Master of Ceremonies* by Thomas Gainsborough（1769）©Fashion Museum Bath

Chapter 2

- *Northanger Abbey* retold by Rimona Calavetta graphic novel com. 2020 版表紙 ©Gaia Marfurt
- "Always arm-in-arm when they walked" *Northanger Abbey* 1907 年版 C. E. Brock による挿絵
- *Bath, Somerset; bathers and onlookers* by W. Elliott after T. Robins ©Science Museum Group
- "The Card-room at Bath" by Hablot K. Browne（1837）from *Pickwick Papers* © Hablot Knight Browne
- "Mr. John Thorpe" *Northanger Abbey* 1907 年版 C. E. Brock による挿絵

Chapter 3

- *Northanger Abbey* Cumulus Publishing 2015 版表紙
- *Fancy Dress Ball at the Bath Assembly Room* by Thomas Rowlandson（1790s）
- *Country Dance* by Thomas Rowlandson（1790s）
- *Portrait of Captain Thomas Coram* by William Hogarth（1740）部分
- *Rosamond, Lady Barrow* by Thomas Lawrence（1826）部分

Chapter 4

- *Northanger Abbey* Audio Audible Book Trout Lake Media 2012 版表紙
- グロスター州を代表する城の一つスゥドリー城 ©Wdejager
- *A self portrait of Carl Joseph Begas*（c.1820）部分
- *Portrait of Jean Thurel* by Antoine Vestier（1788 /1804）部分
- *Northanger Abbey* ジョン・ジョーンズ監督映画 2007 年北米発売 DVD パッケージ

Chapter 5

- *Northanger Abbey* Illustrated and retold by Steven Butler, Fantasticfiction 2020 年度版表紙
- "Anxious attentions to the weather" *Northanger Abbey* 1907 年 版 C. E. Brock による挿絵
- ブレイズ城
- "Pray, pray, stop, Mr. Thorpe!" *Northanger Abbey* 1907 年版 C. E. Brock による挿絵
- 現在のバース王立劇場
- *Royal Theatre of Bath, Orchard Street* by Thomas Rowlandson c.1790
- *Laura Place, Bath*

Chapter 6

- *Northanger Abbey* Norton Critical Edition 2004 年版表紙
- *Portrait of General Peter Mikhailovich Kaptzevich* by George Dawe（1823-1825）部分

- *Lady Taylor* by Thomas Gainsborough（c.1780）部分

Chapter 7

- *Northanger Abbey* Annotated by David M. Shepard Anchor Books 2013 年版表紙
- イギリスで 2013 年に 6 枚セットで発行された Jane Austen Postal Stamps の 1 枚
- "Henry drove so well" *Northanger Abbey* 1904 年版 H. M. Brock による挿絵
- *Northanger Abbey* Annotated and Illustrated Book, Teacher's Edition Walmart Publisher 2020 年版表紙
- *Northanger Abbey* Fadem Bookdoors Publisher 2010 年版 Frank Loudin による表紙

Chapter 8

- *Northanger Abbey* Barnes & Noble Classics 2005 年版表紙
- オステリー・パーク ロバート・アダムによる内装
- 18 世紀製暖炉、ニューヨーク私邸（筆者撮影）
- 古文書 ©Atlantios at Pixabay
- "Catherine opening the chest." *Northanger Abbey*, Jane Austen. J.M. Dent and Co.1895 年版 William C. Cooke による挿絵
- Warwick Castle（筆者撮影）
- "It was my mother's favourite walk" *Northanger Abbey* 1907 年 版 C.E Brock による挿絵
- "It was an air and attitude of Montoni!" *Northanger Abbey* 1907 年版 C.E Brock による挿絵
- シオン・ハウス ロバート・アダムによる内装
- シオン・ハウス ロバート・アダムのデザイン画

Chapter 9

- *Murder at Northanger Abbey: Sequel to Jane Austen's spoof on the Gothic Novel* by Annon Winslow 2020 年版表紙
- *Mrs. Thomas Gainsborough* by Thomas Gainsborough（1777）部分
- *Northanger Abbey* 1833 年版挿絵（出版元不明）
- 19 世紀製天蓋付きベッド ニューヨーク私邸（著者撮影）
- *The Mysteries of Udolpho* by Ann Radcliffe パリ出版 1798 年版挿絵

Chapter 10

- *Northanger Abbey* Clandestine Classics Collection 2012 版表紙
- "Good God! How came you up that staircase?"（ママ）*Northanger Abbey* 1907 年版 C. E. Brock による挿絵
- *Gainsborough Dupont* by Thomas Gainsborough（c.1770-1775）©Tate Britain
- *Northanger Abbey* Wordsworth Classics 2005 版表紙

Chapter 11

- *Northanger Abbey* Bantam Classic 1984 版表紙
- バース近郊の元牧師館（現 B&B 筆者撮影）
- "Mr. and Mrs. Morland's surprise was...considerable" *Northanger Abbey* 1907 年版 C. E. Brock による挿絵
- *Mr. and Mrs. Hallett（The Morning Walk）* by Thomas Gainsborough（1785）©The National Gallery, London
- *Northanger Abbey* dtv 社（ドイツ）2009 年版表紙
- *Northanger Abbey* ジョン・ジョーンズ監督映画 2008 年ロシア発売 DVD パッケージ

注記）出版物表紙、DVD パッケージ、筆者撮影写真以外はすべて wikipedia の public domain もしくは pixabay の free use から引用した。

＜コラムの図について＞

Chapter 1

バース古地図（1610 年）
https://en.wikipedia.org/wiki/Bath,_Somerset#/media/File:Speed_baths.jpg
Public domain

バース　ローマン・バスの遺跡
https://en.wikipedia.org/wiki/Bath,_Somerset#/media/File:Roman_Baths_
c1900_2.jpg Public domain

バース・アビー、ファッサード
https://commons.wikimedia.org/wiki/File:060529-17-BathAbbey.jpg　Author:
Luxborealis

バース・アビー、ファッサード部分「天使の階段」
https://commons.wikimedia.org/wiki/File:Himnastigi.jpg　Author: Haukurth

バース・アビー天井
https://commons.wikimedia.org/wiki/File:Bath_Abbey,_ceiling_-_geograph.
org.uk_-_717407.jpg Author: Brian Robert Marshall

バース、ロイヤル・パヴィリオン
https://commons.wikimedia.org/wiki/File:Brighton_royal_pavilion_Qmin.jpg
Author: Qmin

バース、ロイヤル・パヴィリオン、音楽室天井
https://commons.wikimedia.org/wiki/File:Brighton_Pavilion_（18814891875）.
jpg　Author: Bryan Ledgard

Chapter 2

The Mysteries of Udolpho 1793 年版挿絵
https://upload.wikimedia.org/wikipedia/commons/8/83/
Ilustracja_do_powiesci_Ann_Radcliffe_%22The_Mysteries_of_Udol-
pho%22_1793_%28120174439%29.jpg　Public domain

The Castle of Otranto　ドイツ 1794 年版イラスト
https://commons.wikimedia.org/wiki/File:Houghton_EC75_
W1654_764c%E2%84%93_-_Castle_of_Otranto_ill.jpg　Public domain

Chapter 3

デヴォンシャー邸のギャンブル（デヴォンシャー侯爵夫人ジョージアナが描
かれている）
https://commons.wikimedia.org/wiki/File:Thomas_Rowlandson,_A_
Gambling_Table_at_Devonshire_House_（1791,_detail).jpg　Public Domain

カード・ルームがあったバースの建物
https://commons.wikimedia.org/wiki/File:Fashion_Museum_and_Assembly_
Rooms_Bath.jpg
Author: Mark Anderson

ロバート・アダムのデザインによるセダン・チェア（1775 年制作）
https://commons.wikimedia.org/wiki/File:An_ornate_sedan_chair_with_a_
state_crown_on_top._Engraving_b_Wellcome_V0041108.jpg　Author: Fæ

Beau Nash the Master of Ceremonies Bath under Beau Nash（1907）by Lewis
Merville 表紙部分 ©Michael Maggs
https://commons.wikimedia.org/wiki/Category:Beau_Nash#/media/File:Beau-
Nash.jpg　Public Domain

バースのセンチュリー・カジノ（チェーン店の一つ）（筆者撮影）

Chapter 4

ジェイン・オースティンの時代のダンスの 5 つの基本ポジション
https://en.wikipedia.org/wiki/Regency_dance#/media/File:Five_positions_of_
dancing_Wilson_1811.jpg　Public domain

パンプ・ルームのエッチング（1864）
https://commons.wikimedia.org/wiki/File:Bath_Pump_Room_&_Baths.jpg
Public domain

Chapter 5

ピーター・レリー作《ネル・グイン》（c.1675）
https://upload.wikipedia.org/wikipedia/commons/b/bb/Nell_Gwyn_by_Sir_
Peter_Lely.jpg
https://commons.wikimedia.org/wiki/File:Studio_of_Peter_Lely_-_Unknown_
woman,_formerly_known_as_Nell_Gwyn_-_NPG.jpg
Author: ArtMechanic

トマス・ゲインズバラ作《ディヴィッド・ギャリック》（1770）
https://commons.wikimedia.org/wiki/File:David_Garrick_by_Thomas_
Gainsborough.jpg
Public domain

トマス・ゲインズバラ作《シドンズ夫人》（1785）
https://commons.wikimedia.org/wiki/File:Thomas_Gainsborough_015.jpg
Public domain

トマス・ゲインズバラ作《エリザ・リンリー》（c.1772）部分
https://www.wikiart.org/en/thomas-gainsborough/the-linley-sisters-mrs-
sheridan-and-mrs-tickell-1772　Public domain

シェリダンの代表作の一つ『恋がたき』のバース巡業のチラシ。主演のファ
ニー・ケンブルがシドンズ夫人の妹であることに言及している　©Bodleian
Libraries
https://commons.wikimedia.org/wiki/File:Bodleian_Libraries,_Playbill_of_
Theatre,_Wednesday_Decr._2d-_1795,_announcing_The_rivals,_or,_A_trip_
to_Bath_%26c..jpg　Public domain

バースのロイヤル・クレッセント
https://commons.wikimedia.org/wiki/File:Royal.crescent.aerial.bath.arp.jpg
Public domain

シェリダンと摂政皇太子とその恋愛相手フィッツハーバート夫人の政治的企
みを風刺するエッチング（1791）©National Portrait Gallery
https://upload.wikimedia.org/wikipedia/commons/2/2c/
Bandelures%27_%28King_George_IV%3B_Maria_Anne_
Fitzherbert_%28n%C3%A9e_Smythe%29%3B_Richard_Brinsley_
Sheridan%29_by_Samuel_William_Fores.jpg　Public Domain

Chapter 6

1800 年代、男性の正装の例
https://commons.wikimedia.org/wiki/File:Man%27s_coat_and_vest_with_
metal-thread_embroidery_c._1800.jpg　Public domain

ヴィクトリア＆アルバート博物館所蔵の摂政時代の男性服（筆者撮影）
トマス・ゲインズバラ《ハーボード・ハーボード男爵》（c/1783）
https://commons.wikimedia.org/wiki/File:Thomas_Gainsborough,_Sir_
Harbord_Harbord_1783.jpg　Public Domain

ブランメルの肖像画のエッチング

https://commons.wikimedia.org/wiki/File:BrummellEngrvFrmMiniature.jpg
Public domain

ブランメルの戯画（Richard Dighton 1805）
https://commons.wikimedia.org/wiki/File:BrummellDighton1805.jpg　Public domain

ジョージ四世の戯画　©British Museum
https://commons.wikimedia.org/wiki/File:A_voluptuary_under_the_horrors_of_digestion_（BM_1851,0901.618_1）.jpg　Public domain

ロンドン、ジャーミン通に立つブランメルの像 https://commons.wikimedia.org/wiki/File:Beau_Brummell_Statue_Jermyn_Street.JPG
Photo by Herr uebermann

Chapter 7
イングランドにおける代表的パッラーディオ風建築の一つ、ウォーバーン・アビー
https://commons.wikimedia.org/wiki/File:WoburnAbbey01.JPG　Photo by Chris Nyborg

ハンス・ホルバインによるトマス・クロムウェルの肖像
https://commons.wikimedia.org/wiki/File:Cromwell,Thomas（1EEssex）01.jpg
　Public domain

南ウェールズのティンターン・アビーの廃墟
https://commons.wikimedia.org/wiki/File:Tintern_Abbey_and_Courtyard.jpg
photo by Saffron Blaze

Chapters 8
スティーブントン牧師館
https://commons.wikimedia.org/wiki/File:StevetonRectory.jpg　Public domain

オースティン家　©Genealogy Corner
Genealogy Corner の系図を元に筆者が構成
（参照　https://thegenealogycorner.com/2011/04/01/jane-austens-family-tree/）

ジェインの書き物机　©British Library
Jane Austen's writing desk British library: ref Add MS 86841
Visibility Public

ハリス・ビッグ＝ウィザー
https://www.wikitree.com/photo.php/6/69/Bigg-Wither-2.jpg

トム・ルフロイ
https://en.m.wikipedia.org/wiki/Thomas_Langlois_Lefroy#/media/File%3AThomas_Langlois_Lefroy.jpg

Chapter 9
エドワード・オースティン・ナイト
https://commons.wikimedia.org/wiki/File:EdwardAusten.gif Public domain

エドワードが相続したゴッドマーシャム邸
https://commons.wikimedia.org/wiki/File:Godmersham_（1779）.jpg Public domain

バースのミルソム通（筆者撮影）
バースのパラゴン（筆者撮影）
バースのシドニー・プレイス 4 番地正面（筆者撮影）
バースのシドニー・プレイス 4 番地裏庭（筆者撮影）

Chapter 10
サザンプトンのオールセイント教会
https://commons.wikimedia.org/wiki/File:All_Saints_Church,_Southampton,_1852,_cropped.jpg
Public domain

サザンプトンのハイストリート 1820 年
https://upload.wikimedia.org/wikipedia/en/c/c7/Southampton_High_Street_1839_Drawn_by_GF_Sargent.jpg
https://www.cs.mcgill.ca/~rwest/wikispeedia/wpcd/images/123/12379.jpg.htm#file（wikipedia から引用のサイト）
Public domain

チョートン・ハウス（エドワードの屋敷の一つ）
https://commons.wikimedia.org/wiki/File:Chawton_House_-b.jpg
Author: Charles DP Miller

チョートン・コテッジ（現ジェイン・オースティン博物館）
https://commons.wikimedia.org/wiki/File:Jane_Austen_house_museum.jpg
Author R ferroni2000

チョートン・コテッジの机（筆者撮影）

ウィンチェスターでジェインが滞在した家
https://commons.wikimedia.org/wiki/File:Jane_Austen%27s_House_-_geograph.org.uk_-_1314316.jpg
Author: Peter Trimming

ウィンチェスター大聖堂
https://commons.wikimedia.org/wiki/File:WinCath30Je6-4836wiki.jpg
Author: WyrdLight.com

ジェイン・オースティンの足跡の地図
https://commons.wikimedia.org/wiki/File:Jane_Austen_Map.png
Author: Online Map Creation, Ruhrfisch

Chapter 11
ジェイン・オースティンの肖像のある 10 ポンド紙幣

テキストの音声は、弊社 HP　https://www.eihosha.co.jp/
の「テキスト音声ダウンロード」のバナーからダウンロードできます。
また、下記 QR コードを読み込み、音声ファイルをダウンロードするか、
ストリーミングページにジャンプして音声を聴くことができます。

Northanger Abbey retold in simple English
ノーサンガー・アビー

2023 年 1 月 20 日　初　版

編　著　者 ⓒ 細　川　　　祐　子
発　行　者　　佐　々　木　　　元
発　行　所　株式会社　英　　宝　　社
〒 101-0032 東京都千代田区岩本町 2-7-7
電話 03-5833-5870　FAX03-5833-5872
https://www.eihosha.co.jp/

ISBN 978-4-269-01435-0 C1082
組版・印刷・製本／日本ハイコム株式会社